HOW DO YOU STACK UP?

BOOK OF AGES 30

JOSHUA ALBERTSON
LOCKHART STEELE
JONATHAN VAN GIESON

Copyright © 2003 by
Joshua Albertson, Lockhart Steele, and Jonathan Van Gieson
Illustrations © 2003 by Jonathan Van Gieson

Published by Crown Publishers, New York, New York. Member of the Crown
Publishing Group, a division of Random House, Inc.
www.randomhouse.com

Printed in the United States

Typeset in Gotham and Hoefler Text
with special appearances by Balmoral, Bamboo, Bubbledot, Emblem, Gill Sans,
Intrepid, and Mansour Contour

Book Design by Jonathan Van Gieson
with Joshua Albertson and Lockhart Steele

Library of Congress Cataloging-in-Publication Data
Albertson, Joshua, 1974–
        Book of ages 30 / Joshua Albertson, Lockhart Steele, Jonathan Van
Gieson. — 1st ed.
        1. Young adults—United States—Attitudes. 2. Young adults—United States—
Life skills guides. I. Steele, Lockhart, 1974– II. Van Gieson, Jonathan, 1974– III. Title.

HQ799.7.A43   2003
305.242'0973—dc21   2003055326

ISBN 1-4000-5013-8

10 9 8 7 6 5 4 3 2 1

First Edition

Enjoy www.bookofages.com.

CONTENTS

Lather was thirty years old today,
They took away all of his toys.

—Grace Slick

A Brief Note About Sources
What you are about to read is real. The data in this book—
no matter how absurd it may seem—
was not fabricated, at least not by the authors.
It comes from a wide variety of sources, ranging from
the U.S. Census to www.tina-turner.com.
If you don't believe us, read the endnotes.

30

"The number equivalent to the product of three and ten; ten less than forty..."
—*New Oxford American Dictionary*

YOU ARE

ARE

30

So you're 30. For some, it's no big deal. For others, it's the end of the world. Either way, you're probably wondering, "How do I stack up?"

Fortunately for all of us, Harvard professors have already been over this ground. Around the time you were born, Daniel Levinson identified the "Age Thirty Transition" as the first universally experienced crisis period. "I'm almost 30," the inner refrain goes, "and what have I done with my life?" According to Levinson, a sense of time passing emerges, with more urgency to accomplish something lasting. People are likely to examine their lives to date and judge their achievements—or lack thereof.

That's where *Book of Ages 30* comes in. In the pages that follow, we aim to uncover what it means to be 30—the good, the bad, and the balding.

Maybe you spent your 20s alone, building towers of credit card debt as you roamed the countryside desperately trying to find your third wife, your illegitimate child, and your fifteen minutes of fame. Or maybe you collected millions on your way up the corporate ladder with a supermodel on each arm and Cristal and caviar in your fridge. But were you happy—*really* happy?

No matter what you've been up to, you'll see in *Book of Ages 30* that you're not alone. Sex, drugs, guns, money, Cher—it's all in here.

A NOTE ABOUT CHAPTER INTRODUCTIONS

Introductions are chock-full of random stuff designed to whet your appetite for the upcoming chapter. The chapter quiz will not be graded.

OMITTED DATA

Data: Religion statistics
Reason Omitted: Concerns about apparent underrepresentation of certain religious groups. As a result, a worthy accompanying factoid ("The average age of students graduating from Harvard Divinity School in 2000 was 30") was summarily dismissed.

Data: You are in the second most likely age group to use Linux.
Reason Omitted: Unable to secure rights to penguin logo.

Data: 3% of people in their 30s prefer to have telemarketers call them by their first name.
Reason Omitted: Some people say anything to get off the phone.

CHAPTER QUIZ

1. What do people do more in their early 30s?
a. Drink
b. Watch NASCAR
c. Own a gun
d. Think they're fat

2. TRUE OR FALSE?
The average 30-year-old is more likely to find smoking pot "absolutely wrong" than stealing office supplies.

3. ESSAY QUESTION
Consider the seemingly non-ironic quotation from the Dept. of Labor (p. 13). Drawing on your own experience, attempt to explain what they mean by "the productivity of young workers."

· · · · · · · · WELCOME TO YOUR THIRTIES · · · · · · · · ·

· · · · · You are now **OLDER** than **42%** of America

Don't worry, you're not alone. **3,789,800** Americans will turn 30 this year

15% of Americans are in their 30s

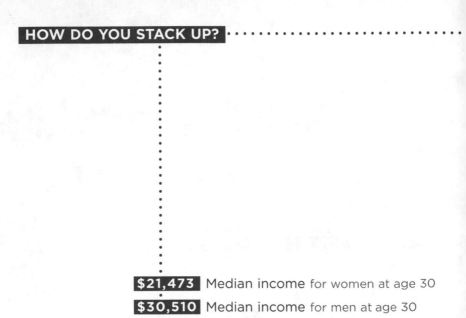

HOW DO YOU STACK UP? ·

$21,473 Median income for women at age 30

$30,510 Median income for men at age 30

Average height for men
in their 30s

5´10.2˝

Average height for women
in their 30s

5´4.6˝

174 LBS.

Average weight for men
of average height

130 LBS.

Average weight for women
of average height

"One might think that by age 30, a typical individual should have settled into a job and completed the transition from school to work. However, past research indicated that at age 30, a substantial percent of workers has been at their job for a very short time."

—*U.S. Dept. of Labor*

43% of 30-year-olds have held their job for 2 years or less

12% report 10 or more years at their current job

"Churning through the labor market, young workers learn about different jobs, and firms learn about the productivity of young workers. Workers can experiment with various types of jobs and eventually decide upon a career." —*U.S. Dept. of Labor*

You've had **7.5 JOBS** in your 30 years

19% have had 3 jobs or less

25% have had more than 10 jobs

You'll have **2.4 JOBS** in the next 5 years

YOU HAVE A **24%** **CHANCE OF** **BEING PROMOTED**
in the next 5 years

30% if you have a bachelor's degree

24% if you have some college but no degree

22% if you only have a high school diploma

20% if you have no diploma

26% if you're a man

23% if you're a woman

36% if you're a man with a bachelor's degree

24% if you're a woman with a bachelor's degree

YOU HAVE A **35%** **CHANCE OF** BEING UNEMPLOYED
in the next 5 years

22% if you have a bachelor's degree

33% if you have some college but no degree

40% if you only have a high school diploma

52% if you have no diploma

If you are unemployed at least once, **expect...**

23% chance of more than 2 spells of unemployment

31% chance of more than 3 spells of unemployment

2.1 average number of spells of unemployment

AGE IS RELATIVE

If you were **A DOG** you would be **210 YEARS OLD**

On **MARS** it's your **SWEET SIXTEEN**

Born on **FEBRUARY 29?** You're only **SEVEN**

"It does change, the age that is young, once in Paris it was twenty-six, then it was twenty-two, then it was nineteen and now it is between thirty and forty. They tell about a new young man, how old is he you say and they say he is thirty." —*Gertrude Stein*

 ••••On **VENUS** you're **49 YEARS OLD** ••••

••In **PARIS** you're **30 YEARS OLD** ••••••••••••••••

•••••On **SATURN** you're a sprightly **ONE YEAR OLD** •••••••

feel they are **46%** in **excellent** health

46% in **good** health

6% in **fair** health

1% in **poor** health

FEELIN' ALRIGHT? **92%** **AIN'T FEELIN' TOO BAD THEMSELVE**

*people in their early 30s
claiming good or excellent health*

IF YOU ATE AN **APPLE A DAY UNTIL YOU TURNED 30**

then

you've

eaten

10,957 **APPLES**

"Anyone over age 30 who is considering a regular exercise program should always consult their physician before they start such a program."
— *"Snow Shoveling Can Be Life-Threatening,"*
Ohio Dept. of Health

······ DROP AND GIVE ME...

Activity	Average	Above Avg.	Excellent
1.5 Mile Run	11:01–12:46	10:00–11:00	< 9:59
Pushups	19–23	24–31	32+
Bench Press*	0.93–1.03	1.04–1.23	1.24+
			for 30-year-olds
1.5 Mile Run	14:24–15:25	12:51–14:23	< 12:50
Pushups	10–21	22–33	34+
Ab Crunches	25–36	37–47	48+

*divide heaviest weight you can lift once by body weight

62% of thirtysomethings
think they are overweight

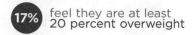
17% feel they are at least
20 percent overweight

of men in their 30s weigh
over 226 pounds **10%** 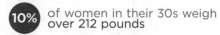 of women in their 30s weigh
over 212 pounds

Q: Isn't it true that fat people are lazy, stupid, weak-willed, lacking
in ambition, selfish, greedy, gluttonous, sedentary, and ugly?

A: No, none of these characterizations have any basis in fact.

—Council on Size & Weight Discrimination FAQ

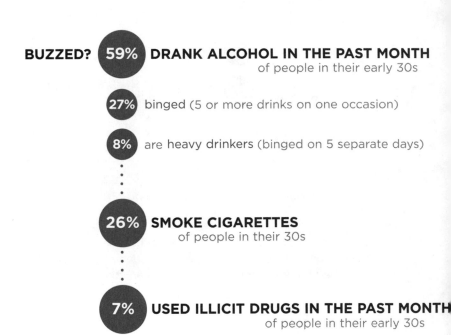

BUZZED? **59%** **DRANK ALCOHOL IN THE PAST MONTH**
of people in their early 30s

27% binged (5 or more drinks on one occasion)

8% are heavy drinkers (binged on 5 separate days)

26% **SMOKE CIGARETTES**
of people in their 30s

7% **USED ILLICIT DRUGS IN THE PAST MONTH**
of people in their early 30s

At the age of 30, 30-year-old Scotch is ripe for the drinking.

YOU'RE GETTING · · · · · · · · · · · · · · · ·

"Psychological health steadily increases from 30
years of age to 40, 50, and 62 years of age."
—*Psychology and Aging, Vol. 15, No. 2*

People in their early 30s say they are  **17%** extremely happy

41% very happy

30% generally satisfied

9% fairly unhappy

3% unhappy most of the time

· ▸ LESS CRAZY

"Three-quarters of persons with schizophrenia develop
the disease between 16 and 25 years of age. Onset is
uncommon after age 30, and rare after age 40."

—*Schizophrenia.com*

YOU ARE ARMED TO THE TEETH •

45% **OF THIRTYSOMETHINGS OWN A FIREARM**

Of those...

23% own all three

31% own a pistol

37% own a shotgun

34% own a rifle

More people in their 30s **own firearms** than those in any other decade of their lives.

Which of these behaviors do you find **ABSOLUTELY WRONG?**

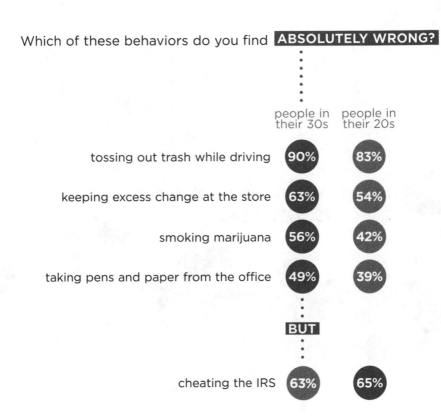

	people in their 30s	people in their 20s
tossing out trash while driving	90%	83%
keeping excess change at the store	63%	54%
smoking marijuana	56%	42%
taking pens and paper from the office	49%	39%
BUT		
cheating the IRS	63%	65%

"It is well for the world that for most of us, by the age of thirty, the character has set like plaster and will never soften again."

—*William James, psychologist and philosopher*

You're watching SLIGHTLY LESS NASCAR

47% in their 30s **watched a race** in the last year

vs. **53%** in their 20s

You're not a HAPPY CAMPER

82% of people who **visit Yosemite** have done so by 30

You're no longer DELUDING YOURSELF ON NEW YEAR'S

26% are **less likely to make a resolution** than those in their 20s

but **26%** are **more likely to keep it**

Chances are, if you have not yet realized **YOU ARE GAY** · · · · ·

You probably **NEVER WILL**

realized they were gay **4%** after age 30

came out of the closet **11%** after age 30

of people over 30 who
identify themselves as gay

FRIES WITH THAT? **13%** **HAVE NO HIGH SCHOOL DIPLOMA**
by their early 30s

33% have a high school diploma but no more

19% have some college but no degree

10% have an associate degree

26% have a bachelor's degree or higher

Americans under 30 are twice as likely to get their news from late-night comedians as Americans over 30.

> "I'm 30 years old, but I read
> at the 34-year-old level."
> —*Dana Carvey*

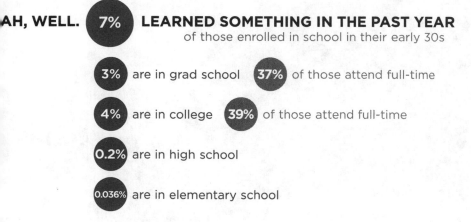

AH, WELL. **7%** **LEARNED SOMETHING IN THE PAST YEAR**
of those enrolled in school in their early 30s

3% are in grad school **37%** of those attend full-time

4% are in college **39%** of those attend full-time

0.2% are in high school

0.036% are in elementary school

78% **OWN A VEHICLE**
of families headed by people under 35

It's worth, on average: **$8,900**

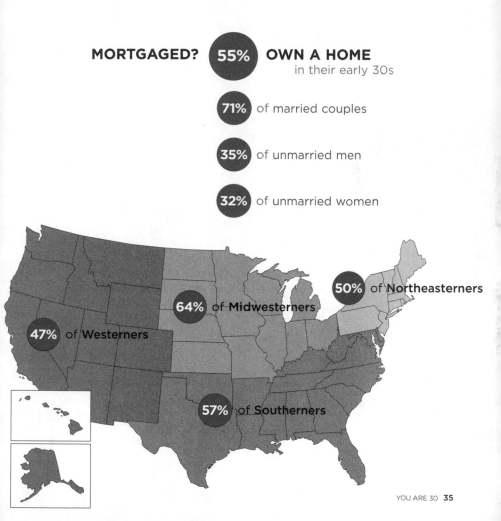

MORTGAGED? **55%** **OWN A HOME**
in their early 30s

71% of married couples

35% of unmarried men

32% of unmarried women

50% of Northeasterners

64% of Midwesterners

47% of Westerners

57% of Southerners

"The only time you really live fully is from thirty to sixty.... The young are slaves to dreams; the old servants of regrets. Only the middle-aged have all their five senses in the keeping of their wits."

—Hervey Allen

LIFE

BEGINS AT

30

There's plenty of evidence to prove that, at 30, you're still on the right side of the curve. Few scholars have brought insight to this concept as effectively as W8Lifter of W8Lifter.com.

"Your 20's were about turning inward, getting out from underneath your parents, and discovering the true you.... Yes, your childhood friends have all grown up, bought town houses, moved away or got married. Yes, your responsibilities as an adult have increased 300 fold.... Now you are 30. It is time to look outward, embrace the world and discover new things and go new places. You are established in who you are. There are a whole lot of new people who want to find out about YOU. So get going. Now is the time to start living."

MOST SHOCKING REVELATION IN THIS CHAPTER
100 - 30 = 70 (p. 44)

LEAST SHOCKING REVELATION
Through hard work and perseverance, Horatio Alger sold his first book (p. 48).

A PAID ADVERTORIAL FROM THE INSURANCE INDUSTRY OF AMERICA
"At age 30, you and a partner can insure yourselves for life for about $900 annually (the minimum premium of a universal life policy for two 30-year-old nonsmokers who wish coverage of $200,000). At age 64, you'll have a fund value of $146,628 in addition to the $200,000 death benefit. Congratulations. You are now ready to die rich."

OMITTED DATA

Data: At age 30, Harriet Tubman made her first trip to the South as a free woman to help bring other slaves to freedom.
Reason Omitted: What the hell do you put on the page opposite that?

Data: The most common age of identity-theft victims is 30.
Reason Omitted: Data stolen.

Data: Grandma Moses had not become a successful painter by the time she was 30.
Reason Omitted: Grandma Moses had not become a successful painter by the time she was 75, either. Why do you think they call her Grandma *Moses*?

CHAPTER QUIZ

1. Which two people were voted sexiest man alive by *People* after they turned 30?
a. Sylvester Stallone & Mr. T
b. George Clooney & Harrison Ford
c. Jesus & Conan O'Brien
d. Jameses Joyce & Naismith

2. TRUE OR FALSE?
By 30, Jesus found Jesus, and asked him WWID?

3. ESSAY QUESTION
Write a successful screenplay.

Turned 30: 5/6/1991
Profession: Handsome
Residence during first year in L.A.: Friend's closet
Year chosen Sexiest Man Alive: 1997
Name of pet pig: Max

GEORGE CLOONEY
PREPPED FOR SURGERY

BUILDUP: 30-year-old George Clooney played a supporting role in the the ABC sitcom *Baby Talk*, one of 15 failed series or pilots he appeared in prior to hitting it big.

BREAKTHROUGH: Perhaps drawing on his experience with infants on the set of *Baby Talk*, Clooney fought for the role of pediatrician Dr. Doug Ross after getting an advance script for the pilot of *ER*. The show premiered when Clooney was 33, and the next year he would garner fame—and an Emmy nomination. Countless questionable movie roles lay ahead.

YOU STILL HAVE TIME TO
BECOME A DOCTOR

One plausible timeline

1 Sweat through pre-med requirements in post-bac program **2 YEARS**

2 Attend medical school **4 YEARS**

3 Open residency envelope **2 MINUTES**

4 Fulfill residency requirement **4 YEARS**

5 Open practice; begin repaying debt

Age at completion
40 YEARS, 2 MINUTES

Turned 30: 7/13/1972
Profession: Superstar
Year chosen Sexiest Man Alive: 1998
According to Luke: "Take care of yourself, Han. I guess that's what you're best at, isn't it?" —*Luke Skywalker, Ep. 4*

HARRISON FORD
WAS A FAIRLY SUCCESSFUL CARPENTER

BUILDUP: Harrison Ford, who always wanted to be an actor, had given up and turned to carpentry until George Lucas cast him in *American Graffiti.* The film was a hit, but the 30-year-old Ford, discouraged by his $500 weekly salary for the part, returned to the more lucrative profession of building stuff.

BREAKTHROUGH: Four years later, Lucas handed the carpenter the part of Han Solo in *Star Wars.* Ford's tool belt disappeared with the Death Star.

Turned 30: 12/25/30
Profession: Superstar
According to Luke: "And Jesus himself began to be about thirty years of age, being (as was supposed) the son of Joseph, which was the son of Heli." —*Luke 3:23*

JESUS OF NAZARETH
LAID DOWN HIS HAMMER

BUILDUP: Jesus of Nazareth gave up the craft of carpentry at age 30 to begin his ministry.

BREAKTHROUGH: Soon afterward, Jesus performed his first miracle, turning water to wine. Note: Biblical scholars take issue with Luke on Jesus' age when he began his work. *Bible Time* observes, "No doubt the author believed himself to be writing about the age of Jesus [at his] baptism. In actual fact [he] was probably about 29 full years old when this happened... [W]e can presume Jesus was 29, 28, 31 or further away just from the structure of this comment."

If you invest **$1,000 A YEAR** starting at age **30** · · · · · · · · ·

One method to **allocate a retirement portfolio**, the "Rule of 100," suggests that you subtract your age from 100. The resulting number is how much of your portfolio should be invested in stocks. For example, at 30 years old, 100 minus 30 equals 70, so 70% of your portfolio should be allocated to stocks, 20% to bonds, and 10% to cash. Wheee!

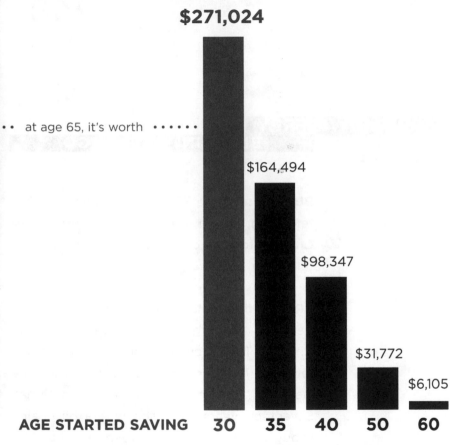

$271,024

at age 65, it's worth

$164,494

$98,347

$31,772

$6,105

AGE STARTED SAVING 30   35   40   50   60

Totals based on 10% rate of return
(This assumes you don't lose it all investing in the next tulip craze.)

Turned 30: 1/29/1984
Profession: DayQuil
Companies owned with "Harpo" in name: Harpo, Inc.; Harpo Productions, Inc.; Harpo Studios, Inc.; Harpo Films, Inc.; Harpo Print, LLC; Harpo Video Inc.
Premiere show guest: Margaret Kent, author, *How to Marry the Man of Your Choice*

OPRAH WINFREY
BLEW INTO CHICAGO

BUILDUP: At age 30, Oprah Winfrey left her television job in Baltimore and moved to Chicago to take over the ailing half-hour TV talk show *AM Chicago.*

BREAKTHROUGH: Within a month, the show became the highest-rated talk show in Chicago. The following year, *AM Chicago* was renamed *The Oprah Winfrey Show.* When she was 32, Oprah's show went national. Seventeen years later, she was a billionaire, though she also bore responsibility for unleashing Dr. Phil on the world.

Turned 30: 4/18/1993
Profession: NyQuil
Hair color: Foolishly red
Height: 7'4" (unconfirmed)
Premiere show guests: John Goodman, Drew Barrymore, Tony Randall

CONAN O'BRIEN
APPALLED TELEVISION CRITICS

BUILDUP: Eight days after his 30th birthday, former *SNL* and *Simpsons* scribe Conan O'Brien was awarded his own late-night talk show on NBC, replacing *Late Night with David Letterman.* Less than five months later, *Late Night with Conan O'Brien* debuted.

BREAKTHROUGH: Soon after, TV critic Tom Shales observed, "Hey, you, Conan O'Brien! Get the heck off TV!... He is jittery, jiggly, giggly, and wobbly." Less than a decade later, O'Brien signed a contract for $8 million a year, making him jittery, jiggly, giggly—and rich.

WRITERS' BLOCKS

hitting the presses after 30

JANE AUSTEN'S
Turned 30: 12/16/1805
LIFE READ LIKE A JANE AUSTEN NOVEL

Unmarried and without prospects, Austen faced financial peril after the death of her father. Relying on her brothers' support, she continued to write fiction and penned her own happy ending with the publication of *Sense and Sensibility* at age 35.

HORATIO ALGER
Turned 30: 1/13/1862
WAS NOT YET A HORATIO ALGER STORY

At 32, Alger would sell his first book, a children's story about a boy who, through perseverance and hard work, rose from poverty to success. Alger spent his life churning out 120 variations on this gripping rags-to-riches theme.

JAMES JOYCE
Turned 30: 2/2/1912
GOT BURNT ON THE EMERALD ISLE

Still unknown at 30, Joyce tried to convince his Irish publisher to print his short-story collection, *Dubliners*. Instead, fearing the book would run afoul of obscenity laws, the publisher burned it. Published in England two years later, *Dubliners* established Joyce's literary career.

KURT VONNEGUT
Turned 30: 11/11/1952
WAS BOOKING AUTOMOBILE SALES

Vonnegut had his first novel, *Player Piano,* on the shelves at age 30. The work, however, was dismissed by critics as "mere science fiction." Vonnegut spent his 30s working at a school for disturbed students and managing a Saab dealership before the publication of *Cat's Cradle* a decade later brought his work to a wider audience.

ANNE RICE
Turned 30: 10/4/1971
HADN'T SUNK HER TEETH IN

A year after her daughter succumbed to leukemia, the still-despondent 31-year-old Rice sought solace in words. In five weeks, she turned a short story she'd written, "Interview with the Vampire," into a novel. Published in 1976, the novel became her breakthrough work.

AMY TAN
Turned 30: 2/19/1982
WAS SHIT OUT OF LUCK

During a counseling session for workaholism, the 33-year-old Tan noticed her therapist had fallen asleep—for the third time. She promptly quit therapy and joined a fiction-writing workshop. Four years later, her first novel, *The Joy Luck Club,* sold its first of more than two million copies.

Turned 30: 10/15/1989
Profession: Celebrity chef
Maximum distance allowed to kick it up (by law): A notch
Actual plot, first episode of NBC sitcom *Emeril:* Network bosses force Emeril to start cooking low-calorie food, inciting hungry fans to riot

EMERIL LAGASSE
KICKED IT UP A NOTCH

"Music, dancing, fencing, painting, and mechanics possess professors under the age of twenty years, but pre-eminence in cookery can never be attained under thirty years of age."
—*Ude, chef to Louis XIV*

BUILDUP: Five months after his 30th birthday, Emeril's first restaurant, Emeril's Restaurant, opened in New Orleans. BAM! It was named "Best New Restaurant of the Year" by *Esquire.*

BREAKTHROUGH: Four years later, Emeril's new cooking show, *Essence of Emeril,* debuted on the Food Network. By the end of his 30s, Emeril had authored five cookbooks, owned six restaurants, and was in the process of developing a sitcom for NBC, which would—BAM!—be cancelled after seven episodes.

YOU STILL HAVE TIME TO
BECOME A CHEF & OWN A RESTAURANT

One plausible timeline (based on the early career of Emeril Lagasse as described on Emerils.com) • • • • • • •

1 Work at a Portuguese bakery to "master the art of bread and pastry baking" **SEVERAL MONTHS**

2 "Turn down a music scholarship" to earn a doctorate in Culinary Arts **6 YEARS**

3 Travel to Paris to "polish your skills and learn the art of classic French cuisine" **3 MONTHS**

4 "Practice your art at several fine restaurants" in New York, Boston, Philadelphia **4 YEARS**

5 Be "lured to New Orleans" **3 HOURS, 30 MIN.** (direct flight from New York)

6 "Establish your star" by serving as executive chef at "legendary restaurant" **7.5 YEARS**

7 Open eponymous restaurant in "the chic Warehouse District in downtown New Orleans" or other convenient location

• Age at completion:

47 YEARS, 9 MONTHS, 3.5 HOURS

Turned 30: 11/30/1865
Profession: Mustachioed humorist
Other résumé lines: River pilot, miner
Reason forced to leave Nevada in 1864: Broke dueling laws
Patent: "Self-pasting" scrapbook

MARK TWAIN
HAD A FROG UP HIS SLEEVE

BUILDUP: On the day of his 30th birthday, Samuel Langhorne Clemens found himself unemployed in San Francisco. A few months earlier, he'd left his job at a local newspaper.

"It was fearful drudgery—soulless drudgery—and almost destitute of interest. It was an awful slavery for a lazy man."

—*Mark Twain*

BREAKTHROUGH: Unknown to Clemens, 12 days previously the *Saturday Press* in New York City had printed a short story of his (under the pen name Mark Twain) that would later come to be called "The Celebrated Jumping Frog of Calaveras County." Response to the story won Twain nationwide acclaim and launched his fiction-writing career.

Turned 30: 2/18/1961
Profession: Non-mustachioed non-humorist
Original first name: Chloe
Reason changed: Too many people mispronounced it
Number of Oprah's Book Club books: 4

TONI MORRISON
WAS NOT YET BELOVED

BUILDUP: Seeking an escape from an unhappy marriage, 30-year-old Toni Morrison joined a writers group at Howard University, where she taught English. One of her stories concerned a black girl who prayed for blue eyes.

BREAKTHROUGH: At 33, having left Howard and her husband, she took a job as an editor at Random House. She dusted off the short story and turned it into her first novel, *The Bluest Eye*. Thirty years later, Morrison's work had bewildered countless high school English students—and won her the Nobel Prize in Literature.

Turned 30: 5/21/1982
Profession: 20th letter of the alphabet
Former profession: Bodyguard for Muhammad Ali, Diana Ross, Michael Jackson
Height: Shorter than you'd think
Crime-solving cartoon buddies: Teenage gymnasts

MR. T ·
WAS PITILESS

BUILDUP: A bouncer and personal bodyguard for most of his 20s, Mr. T made the leap to the big screen when Sylvester Stallone noticed him on a "World's Toughest Bouncer" segment of a TV show and cast him as the villain in *Rocky III.* The movie hit theaters when T was 30.

BREAKTHROUGH: The role paved the way for Mr. T's casting on the NBC show *The A-Team* the following year. There, he would pity fools on a weekly basis, turning a throwaway line from *Rocky III* into the foundation for an entire · · show-business career.

• • "I'm talented and flexible. I could play Hamlet,
even though I look like King Kong." —*Mr. T*

SPORTING CHANCE

lacing 'em up after 30

MICHAEL LEWIS Turned 30: 11/14/2001
NEW ORLEANS SAINTS

BREAKTHROUGH: At 30, Lewis stopped delivering beer for a living and started delivering hits as a special-teams player for the New Orleans Saints. A year later he became the first player since 1977 to run back both a kickoff and a punt for touchdowns in one game.

CHUCK SMITH Turned 30: 10/21/1999
FLORIDA MARLINS

BREAKTHROUGH: A 30-year-old career minor leaguer, Smith made it to the big leagues as a pitcher for the Florida Marlins. His teammates wondered what took so long. "You don't usually see a 30-year-old stuck in the minors for ten years with that type of stuff," said Marlin outfielder Cliff Floyd.

CLAY BELLINGER Turned 30: 11/18/1998
NEW YORK YANKEES

BREAKTHROUGH: When the Yankees decided to add 30-year-old rookie Bellinger to their opening-day roster in 1999, coach Don Zimmer delivered the news. "When I finally told him he made the club, he cried and I cried with him," Zimmer said. Bellinger made his playoff debut later that season.

Turned 30: 11/6/1891
Profession: Hoop dreamer
Rule no. 1: "The ball may be thrown in any direction with one or both hands."
On the need for his invention: "We tried to play football indoors, but broke the arms and legs of the players.... We then tried soccer, but broke all the windows."

JAMES NAISMITH
PRACTICED WHAT HE PEACHED

BUILDUP: In 1891, 30-year-old James Naismith was teaching physical education in Springfield, Massachusetts, when his boss asked him to come up with an indoor game that would amuse his students during the cold winter.

BREAKTHROUGH: Fourteen days later, Naismith nailed a couple of peach baskets to the wall and introduced "basket ball" to the class. The invention didn't make Naismith rich, but it did earn him a trip to Berlin in 1936, where he introduced the sport to the Olympic stage.

YOU STILL HAVE TIME TO
BECOME A SUCCESSFUL SCREENWRITER ···

··· Two plausible timelines ···

1 Write screenplay **6 MONTHS**

2 Shop screenplay **6 MONTHS**

3 Get lucky **1 DAY**

················ Age at completion

31 YEARS, 1 DAY

1 Write screenplay **6 MONTHS**

2 Shop screenplay **6 MONTHS**

3 Get waiter job to "tide you over" while revising screenplay **1 YEAR**

4 Wait more tables while shopping screenplay and making five more revisions **10 YEARS**

5 Put screenplay aside "for the time being" to focus on waiting tables **5 YEARS**

··············Age at which promoted to restaurant manager

47 YEARS

Turned 30: 7/6/1976
Profession: Marble-mouthed actor
Blondest wife: Brigitte Nielsen
Salary for *The Party at Kitty and Stud's* (1970): $200
Salary for *Rocky IV* (1985): $15 million

SYLVESTER STALLONE
GOT UP OFF THE MAT

BUILDUP: Early in his career, Sylvester Stallone struggled through a series of rejections and bit parts, including the role of "Stud" in the 1970 porn film *The Party at Kitty and Stud's.*

BREAKTHROUGH: Stallone wrote *Rocky* in three days and sold it for a small fee with the stipulation that he would star in the picture. The movie grossed $100+ million and won the Academy Award for Best Picture. For the 30-year-old Sly, it was a gift that kept giving. After a couple of flops, he returned to the ring at 32 in *Rocky II.* And then again in *III.* And *IV.* And *V.*

"I have always looked to about thirty as the barrier of any real or fierce delight in the passions."

—Lord Byron

LOVE & SEX AT 30

Good news—you're still getting some. According to our research, thirtysomethings are just as active in the bedroom as twentysomethings.

With that little concern out of the way, the question left for academics to confront is, In which *ways* are you still getting it? For one answer, consider the writings of noted sexologist Alfred Kinsey. In his landmark 1953 report *Sexual Behavior in the Human Female*, he observed, "Considering the physiology of sexual response and the mammalian backgrounds of human behavior, it is not so difficult to explain why a human animal does a particular thing sexually. It is more difficult to explain why each and every individual is not involved in every type of sexual activity."

MOST SHOCKING REVELATION

Chris O'Donnell still has a career (pp. 70–71).

LEAST SHOCKING REVELATION

Liz Taylor was not a virgin at 30… and neither was Chester A. Arthur (p. 82).

SEXUAL POSITIONS SUGGESTED BY THIS CHAPTER'S STICK-FIGURE ICONS

"The Peacock" (p. 75)
"The Elephant" (p. 79)
"One in the Chimney" (p. 69)

OMITTED DATA

Data: 73% of women in their early 30s currently use contraception, 21% are sterilized, 21% use the pill, 13% currently use condoms, 1% use implants, 1% use injectables, 1% use IUDs, 2% use diaphragms, 2% use periodic abstinence, 2% use withdrawal, and 8% are sleeping with sterilized men.

Reason Omitted: Underrepresentation of female condom offensive; statistics on male sterilization intimidating.

Data: Reprint of *New York Times* news story about Marilyn Monroe/Arthur Miller nuptials, including the text, "Ms. Monroe wore a sweater and a skirt but no hat. Mr. Miller wore a blue suit and a white shirt but no tie."

Reason Omitted: Copyright tiff.

Cut: Circumcision data.

CHAPTER QUIZ

1. How many times, on average, are people in their 30s having sex per week?

a. 1

b. 2

c. 2.24

d. 3

2. TRUE OR FALSE?
More 30-year-old women have slept with zero partners than have lived with three different partners.

3. ESSAY QUESTION
In Kafka's *The Metamorphosis,* a man turns into a giant bug. As noted on p. 83, Kafka got engaged to his secretary to prove to his father that he was "normal." But can writing stories about men turning into giant bugs be considered normal?

"I'm turning 30 this year. And you know the saying, a woman over 30 is more likely to get hit by an A bomb than find a man."

—*Fanny Fink in* Keiner Liebt Mich *(Nobody Loves Me)*

men single in their early 30s **30%** •

· **20%** women single in their early 30s

"I'm sorry, if a man is over 30 and single, there's something wrong with him. It's Darwinian—they're being weeded out from propagating the species."
—*Miranda in* Sex and the City

SUN	MON	TUES	
✗ 30	31	1	
6	**YOU ARE** GETTIN' IT ON · · · · · · · · · · · · 8 · · · · · 7	✗	
13	✗ 14	15	
✗ 20	21	✗ 22	

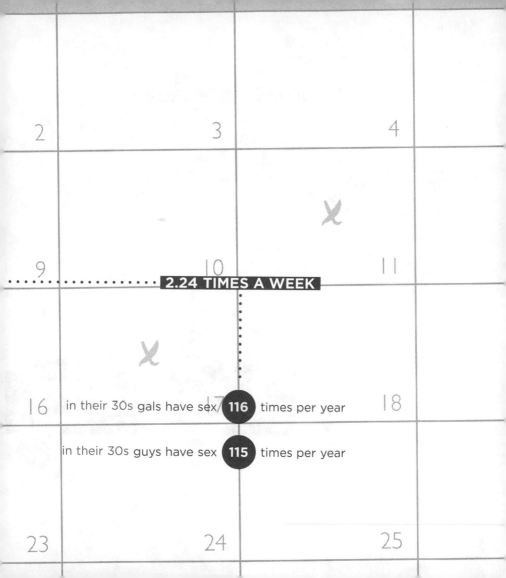

2   3   4

9   10   11

2.24 TIMES A WEEK

16   in their 30s gals have sex **116** times per year   17   18

in their 30s guys have sex **115** times per year

23   24   25

YOU ARE SHACKING UP

women in their early 30s
have lived with 0 partners **11%** · · · · · · · · 1 partner **59%** ·

"No young girl may live alone. Even though she has a father, unless he devotes his entire time to her, she must also have a resident chaperon who protects her reputation until she is married or old enough to protect it herself—which is not until she has reached a fairly advanced age, of perhaps thirty years or over if she is alone, or twenty-six or so if she lives in her father's house and behaves with such irreproachable circumspection that Mrs. Grundy is given no chance to set tongues wagging."

—*Emily Post,* Etiquette, *1922*

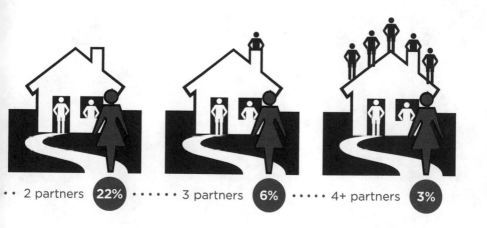

•• 2 partners **22%** •••••• 3 partners **6%** ••••• 4+ partners **3%**

THE BACHELOR

In order to get his share of his deceased grandfather's fortune, Jimmie Shannon (Chris O'Donnell) must marry by 6:05 p.m. on his 30th birthday. Trouble is, his girlfriend just skipped town and his birthday is tomorrow. (New Line Cinema, 1999)

1 in 33 30-year-old men is a virgin

1 in 25 30-year-old women is a virgin

Number of male
SEXUAL PARTNERS
by 30 **FOR WOMEN**

25%
1 partner

14% 2 partners

3 partners **11%**

10% 4 partners

9%
5 partners

6–9 partners **11%**

15% 10+ sexual partners

14%
1 partner

Number of female
SEXUAL PARTNERS
FOR MEN by 30

7% 2 partners

3 partners **8%**

7% 4 partners

7%
5 partners

6–9 partners **13%**

10+ sexual partners **39%**

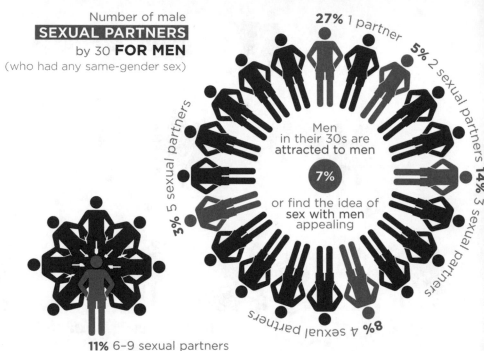

Number of male
SEXUAL PARTNERS
by 30 **FOR MEN**
(who had any same-gender sex)

27% 1 partner

5% 2 sexual partners

14% 3 sexual partners

Men
in their 30s are
attracted to men

7%

or find the idea of
sex with men
appealing

8% 4 sexual partners

3% 5 sexual partners

11% 6-9 sexual partners

32% 10+ sexual partners

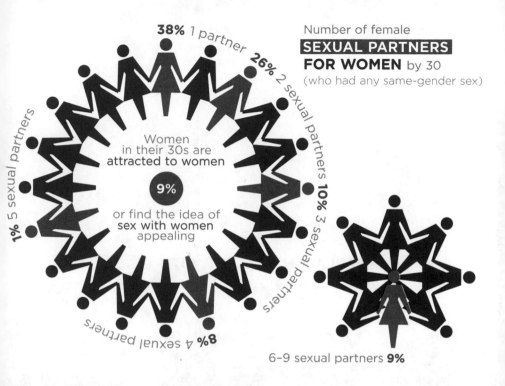

38% 1 partner

26% 2 sexual partners

Number of female
SEXUAL PARTNERS
FOR WOMEN by 30
(who had any same-gender sex)

Women
in their 30s are
attracted to women

9%

or find the idea of
sex with women
appealing

10% 3 sexual partners

1% 5 sexual partners

8% 4 sexual partners

6–9 sexual partners **9%**

10+ sexual partners **9%**

"Yes, that's correct, twenty thousand different ladies. At my age, that equals out to having sex with 1.2 women a day, every day since I was fifteen years old."

—*Wilt Chamberlain,* A View from Above

So, by his 30th birthday,

CHAMBERLAIN HAD SLEPT WITH 6,570 WOMEN

(15 years [ages 15–29] x 365 days/year x 1.2 women/day)

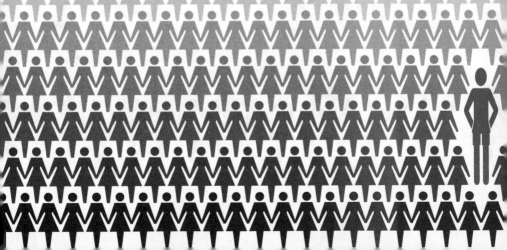

You're ready to start

HAVING SEX WITH `19 MILLION ELEPHANTS`

"The elephant is reckoned the slowest breeder of all known animals, and I have taken some pains to estimate its probable minimum rate of natural increase; it will be safest to assume that it begins breeding when thirty years old, and goes on breeding till ninety years old, bringing forth six young in the interval, and surviving till one hundred years old; if this be so, after a period of from 740 to 750 years there would be nearly nineteen million elephants alive, descended from the first pair."

—*Charles Darwin,* On the Origin of Species

(On the other hand, we may have misinterpreted Darwin's Theory.)

HITCHED? · · · · · · · · · · **81%** **HAVE BEEN MARRIED** · · · · · · ·
women by their early 30s

69% married **once**

11% married **twice**

1% married **three or more times**

DITCHED? · · · · · · · · · · **16%** **HAVE BEEN DIVORCED** · · · · · ·

"Bring a wife home to your house when you are of the right age, not far short of 30 years, nor much above; this is the right time for marriage."
—Hesiod, c. 8th century B.C.

71% **HAVE BEEN MARRIED**
men by their early 30s

62% married once

8% married twice

1% married three or more times

16% **HAVE BEEN DIVORCED**

ALTARED STATES
engaged, married, or divorced at 30

LIZ TAYLOR
Turned 30: 2/27/1962
FINISHED HUSBAND NUMBER FOUR

The Hollywood star, wed for the first time at 18, was on her fourth husband, singer Eddie Fisher. "Eddie and I are going to honeymoon for 40 years," she once said. But soon after turning 30, Taylor began filming *Cleopatra* with Richard Burton and immediately began an affair with him. He would have the honor of serving as her fifth and sixth husbands (out of an eventual haul of eight).

ADAMS, PIERCE, HAYES & ARTHUR
FOUND THEIR FIRST LADIES

John Quincy Adams (6th president), Franklin Pierce (14th president), Rutherford B. Hayes (19th president), and Chester A. Arthur (21st president) all tied the knot when they were 30. Hail to the chiefs!

MADONNA
Turned 30: 8/16/1988
CLOSED HER HEART TO SEAN PENN

Madonna's three-year marriage to Sean Penn was on the rocks as the pop superstar turned 30. For a time it looked like reconciliation was in the cards—she even withdrew the divorce papers. But later that year she filed for divorce for a second, and final, time. Before turning 31, Madonna released the album *Like a Prayer,* creating enough fresh controversy to make her divorce old news.

MARILYN MONROE
Turned 30: 6/1/1956
DIDN'T CATCH THE SEVEN-YEAR ITCH

Twenty-eight days after turning 30, Monroe tied the knot with playwright Arthur Miller, a man ten years her senior. It was Monroe's third, and weirdest, marriage, but it did not halt her increasing dependence on drugs and alcohol. Less than five years later, the couple divorced, and Monroe died the following year at 36.

FRANZ KAFKA
Turned 30: 7/3/1913
FOUND LOVE TO BE A TRIAL

On his 30th birthday, Kafka revealed to his mother that he was engaged. He'd proposed to Felice Bauer, a secretarial assistant, a few months earlier. Some say Kafka wanted to marry to prove to his father that he was "normal." The relationship lasted five years and resulted in two broken engagements, but the despair spurred Kafka on. Between 29 and 33, he wrote most of his major works.

27%

of women in their early 30s don't use contraception

What a coincidence!

visited a health-care provider for a pregnancy test in the last year

17% one pregnancy

26% two pregnancies

19% three pregnancies

21% four or more pregnancies

TEST CAME UP BLUE?  **83%** **HAVE EVER BEEN PREGNANT**
by their early 30s

BABY ON BOARD!

5.6% **ARE PREGNANT OR POSTPARTUM**
in their early 30s

6% are trying to get pregnant

8% expect never to have children

0.5% have adopted a child

1% are looking to adopt

You're having **MORE BABIES** in your 30s · · · · · · · · · · · · ·

························· than your **MOTHER**

births per 1,000 women ages 30–34 **94** in 2000

births per 1,000 women ages 30–34 **52** in 1975

"Bureaucrats: they are dead at 30 and buried at 60. They are like custard pies; you can't nail them to a wall."

—*Frank Lloyd Wright*

MONEY & POWER AT 30

Not everybody is rich and powerful by 30, but in one way or another, we're all sought after.

As your collection agent notes, "Dear Friend, this claim has been turned over to our office for collection. I want to let you know that we intend to pursue this claim and reserve the right to report this matter to the credit bureau, as well as pursue other remedies. Should it be economically feasible, that would include litigation. I fully realize that you may contest the merits of this claim. Certainly, it is not my intent to threaten or alarm you about this matter. I would hope that you take a moment and seriously consider the consequences of your actions. Contacting our office to remedy the situation may prove to be a wise move."

MOST SHOCKING REVELATION
George W. Bush was not always the well-spoken gentleman he is today (p. 109).

LEAST SHOCKING REVELATION
Edward Bok has written a book about himself (p. 95).

CHAPTER-TITLE TRANSLATIONS
dinero y energía
geld und energie
argent et puissance
soldi ed alimentazione
dinheiro e poder
(*Note:* Google's translation engine may have misinterpreted the word "power.")

OMITTED DATA

Data: Biographical details of Sacagawea at age 30.
Reason Omitted: Feared overexposure due to her presence on $1 coin. Also, died at 22.

Data: Decades before she worked for the Clinton administration, Madeleine Albright spent her 30th birthday as a graduate student at Columbia University. In 1968, she completed her master's thesis, "The Soviet Diplomatic Service: Profile of an Elite."
Reason Omitted: Unbearably dull.

Data: U.S. presidents-to-be who were 30 years old when their fathers died.
Reason Omitted: Who cares?

CHAPTER QUIZ

1. Who was a Democrat at 30?
a. Clarence Thomas
b. Elizabeth Dole
c. John Ashcroft
d. Fidel Castro

2. TRUE OR FALSE?
Steve Case still seems somewhat relevant.

3. ESSAY QUESTION:
You are not a millionaire. Explain.

$233,982,000 . . . .

Estimated net worth of Bill Gates on the day of
Microsoft's IPO, March 13, 1986. Mr. Gates was
30 years, four months, and 16 days old.

"But at 30 years of age it is not good for anyone, no matter how well balanced, to have things come his way too fast and too consistently."
—Edward William Bok,
The Americanization of Edward Bok

WORN OUT? 61 YEARS **AVERAGE EXPECTED RETIREMENT AGE**
for people in their 30s

41% HAVE SET UP RETIREMENT ACCOUNTS ··
of families headed by people under 35

· median value **$6,400**

20% **own** savings bonds · · · · · median value **$500**

11% **own** stocks · · · · · · · · · · median value **$3,200**

23% **own** life insurance · · · · · median value **$3,700**

8% **own** mutual funds · · · · · median value **$5,800**

$1,000,000

25% of college students think they'll be millionaires by 30

$65,900

mean net worth for families headed by people under 35

•••• that's **$934,100** short of a million

Reginald Istrant
190 Barbour Street
Providence, R.I. 02910

Dear Mr. Istrant,

This claim has been turned over to our office for collection. I want to let you know that the Hide/Seek Collection Agency intends to pursue this claim and reserve the right to report this matter to the Credit Bureau, as well as pursue other remedies. Should it be economically feasible, that would include litigation.

The process of litigation has not yet been instituted. If it happens, it will be pursued in accordance with state statutes. Should a Judgment be issued against you, it will be pursued by a local attorney in your area. You may be charged with court costs, and, in some cases, attorney fees. After a Judgment is issued a creditor has a number of methods available as a result of this process. It might be valuable for you to check the laws in your State pertaining to the Judgment.

I fully realize that you may contest the merits of this claim. Certainly I don't wish to threaten or alarm you about this matter. I would hope that you take the time to consider the consequences of your actions.

Contacting our office to remedy the situation may prove to b

DROWNING? **81%** **CARRY DEBT** of families headed by people under 35

· median balance **$19,200**

51% **have a** credit-card balance · · · median balance **$1,500**

60% **have an** installment loan · · · · · median balance **$9,100**

33% **have a** mortgage · · · · · · · · · · median balance **$71,000**

YOU ARE LESS LIKELY TO FALL ASLEEP AT YOUR DESK · ·

53% of 18- to 29-year-olds report substantial daytime sleepiness

33% of over-30-year-olds report substantial daytime sleepiness

···SADLY, YOUR BOSS DOESN'T CARE

expect only a **2.4%** annual raise over the next 5 years

Turned 30: 8/3/1971
Profession: Embattled MSO matriarch
Former profession: Model

MARTHA STEWART
WAS SELLING LOTS OF STOCK

AT 30: Stewart was a Wall Street stockbroker. Two years later, she purchased an old farmhouse in Connecticut with her husband. She supervised its restoration and launched a custom catering business, starting her on the path to becoming a home-life media mogul.

..MSO 11 1/16 DN 1/8..

"We'd be holding a cooking class in my kitchen... and Martha would constantly interrupt what I'd been saying and announce that I wasn't doing something right... And I'd just stand there dumbstruck at her rudeness, and the class would come to an end, and she'd sweep up her things and leave."
—*Norma Collier, Martha's first catering partner*

Turned 30: 8/21/1988
Profession: Ousted AOL patriarch
Born and raised: Hawaii

STEVE CASE
TOOK A QUANTUM LEAP

AT 30: Case was running Quantum Computer Services, a company he co-founded at 27. At 31, he renamed Quantum's online services, and America Online was born. Ten years later, he signaled the end of the Internet era by buying Time Warner and running it into the ground.

.....AOL 14 5/8 DN 1/4.....

"When I met Steve he was 30 years old, and he already had a messianic vision of a connected world where the Internet was going to be part of daily life in every way imaginable."

—*Ken Novack, former AOL vice chairman*

YOU STILL HAVE TIME TO GET ON THE BALLOT · · · · · · · · · · · · ·

"No person shall be a Senator who shall not
have attained to the Age of thirty Years."
—*U.S. Constitution, Article 1, Section 3*

by age 30 • • • •

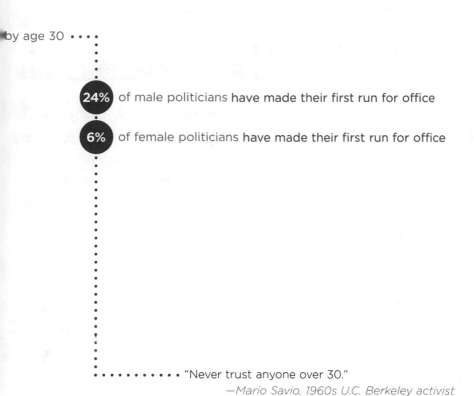

24% of male politicians **have made their first run for office**

6% of female politicians **have made their first run for office**

"Never trust anyone over 30."
—*Mario Savio, 1960s U.C. Berkeley activist*

Turned 30: 8/19/1976
Profession: 42nd president
Office pets: Socks (cat), Buddy (dog), Monica (woman)

BILL CLINTON
MADE LOVE TO ARKANSAS VOTERS

AT 30: In the middle of an on-again/off-again love affair with Arkansas voters, Bill Clinton was elected the state's attorney general at age 30. It was his first elected position. Two years earlier, the newly minted Yale Law School grad had lost a bid for Congress. After two years as attorney general, Clinton was elected governor. He lost his re-election bid at 34, only to win the office back when he was 36.

Turned 30: 7/6/1976
Profession: 43rd president
Office pets: Spot (dog), Barney (dog), India (cat), Ofelia (longhorn)

GEORGE W. BUSH
WAS UNDER THE INFLUENCE

AT 30: George W. Bush was busted for drunk driving. He pleaded guilty to misdemeanor charges of driving under the influence, was fined $150, and had his driving privileges suspended. A year before the incident, he earned his MBA at Harvard and returned to Texas to follow his dad into the oil business. Bush acknowledges that when he was 30 he was "drinking and carousing and fumbling around."

STARS EARN THEIR STRIPES
politicians at 30

JOSEPH McCARTHY
Turned 30: 11/14/1938
HAD SOME SENSE OF DECENCY

At 30, McCarthy became the youngest circuit judge ever elected in Wisconsin. Fourteen years later, he accused most Americans of being Communists.

JOHN ASHCROFT
Turned 30: 5/9/1972
LET THE EAGLE SINK

Ashcroft first ran for public office at age 30, narrowly losing a Republican congressional primary. Nearly 30 years later, after losing a Senate race to a dead man, he was confirmed as George W. Bush's attorney general.

JOHN F. KENNEDY
Turned 30: 5/29/1947
WAS NO JOHN F. KENNEDY

Happy birthday, Mr. President. Kennedy, a decorated WWII veteran, had just entered the House of Representatives at 30. He served for six years before moving on to bigger things—the Senate, the presidency, and Marilyn Monroe.

CLARENCE THOMAS
Turned 30: 6/23/1978
HAD NO ANTS IN HIS PANTS

Future Supreme Court Justice Thomas was an attorney in the pesticide and agriculture division of the Monsanto Company when he was 30. His experience in extermination would serve him well as a death-penalty advocate on the High Court.

ELIZABETH DOLE
Turned 30: 7/29/1966
RAN WITH THE DONKEYS

Fresh out of Harvard Law School, 30-year-old Democrat Elizabeth Hanford landed her first job in the capital, in the Department of Health, Education and Welfare. At 31, she worked in LBJ's White House. By 40, she had switched parties and married Bob Dole.

JOE BIDEN
Turned 30: 11/20/1972
DIDN'T YET HAVE COPIER PRIVILEGES

At 30, Biden became the youngest person to enter the Senate since Rush Dew Holt was elected in 1934. This Delaware Democrat still serves today. His state is small, but his heart is big!

Turned 30: 12/26/1923
Profession: Ruthless dictator
Abandoned careers: Law enforcement, business, teaching

MAO TSE-TUNG
DOLED OUT DETENTION

AT 30: The future leader of Communist China was large and in charge, roaming the halls as the principal of an elementary school in the Hunan province. The job paid the bills while Mao organized to brew class uprising. (Three years earlier, he had been one of just 12 delegates at the first national meeting of the Chinese Communist Party.) At 34, he led a group of peasants into the mountains. The group grew into the Red Army, which would propel him to power following World War II.

"If at age 20 you are not a Communist then you have no heart. If at age 30 you are not a capitalist then you have no brains."
—*attributed to George Bernard Shaw*

Turned 30: 8/13/1956
Profession: Ruthless dictator
At 21: Nasty curveball; scouted by Pittsburgh Pirates

FIDEL CASTRO
GOT CLOSE, BUT NO CIGAR

AT 30: Castro launched his second attempt to overthrow the military government of Cuba. Like his first effort, which landed him in jail for three years, the attack failed miserably—only 12 of the 82 insurgents survived. But Castro was undeterred. Flush with capital from earlier fund-raising efforts in the United States and Mexico, he retreated to the mountains and rebuilt his forces. Three years later, his army of 800 pounded the government into submission. The revolutionaries claimed Havana on New Year's Day 1959, when Castro was 32.

THEY SHOOK UP THE WORLD

international leaders at 30

 MARGARET THATCHER | **Turned 30:** 10/13/1955
WAS NOT YET A MILK SNATCHER

Thatcher was settling into the life of a barrister after failing twice to win election to Parliament. At age 34, she would run again and win, launching her political career. She did not become "Thatcher, milk snatcher" until age 46, when she ended the U.K. free-milk school program.

WM. THE CONQUEROR | **Turned 30:** 1057
WAS BIGGER THAN THE KING

At 30, William the Conqueror was chilling in France. A mere duke at the time, he had fought a series of battles that made him master of his province, able to bid defiance to the king. In 1066, at age 39, he sailed to England and conquered, as he was prone to do.

NAPOLEON | **Turned 30:** 8/15/1799
WAS ON THE VERGE OF A COMPLEX

Two months after Bonaparte's 30th birthday, he seized power in France in a coup d'etat, appointing himself First Council in the Triumvirate—effectively a dictator. At age 35, he named himself emperor.

QUEEN ISABELLA
Turned 30: 4/22/1481
EXPECTED THE SPANISH INQUISITION

When she turned 30, Queen Isabella was busy expelling Jews and Muslims from Spain. A year earlier, she and her husband, Ferdinand, had introduced the Inquisition to her country. Eleven years later, she bankrolled Christopher Columbus's trip to the New World.

NELSON MANDELA
Turned 30: 7/18/1948
BROUGHT SOME LIFE TO THE PARTY

Mandela, at 30, was transforming the African National Congress into a party for the masses. After watching the National Party win South Africa's 1948 elections on an apartheid platform, Mandela and the ANC's Youth League advocated for boycotts, strikes, and civil disobedience in order to bring full citizenship and direct representation to all South Africans.

MIKHAIL GORBACHEV
Turned 30: 3/2/1961
CLIMBED THE RED LADDER

At 30, Mikhail Gorbachev was working his way up the ranks of the local Communist Party. By the end of the decade, he was the party boss to the more than two million people in the Stavropol region. Despite his status as local star, his blotchy head wouldn't reach national prominence until he was well into his 40s.

"Nothing else is new except my cold."
—*Pablo Picasso, age 30*

THIRTY
METER

Think of it as the fuel gauge of life. Our patented ThirtyMeter device measures, by means of a complex mathematical formula, a person's accomplishments at 30 against achievements over the rest of their lives. Some of the people in this chapter were running on fumes at 30; others had just filled up at the gas station of fame... maybe for the last time. How full is your tank? ThirtyMeter knows.

HOW TO READ THE THIRTYMETER

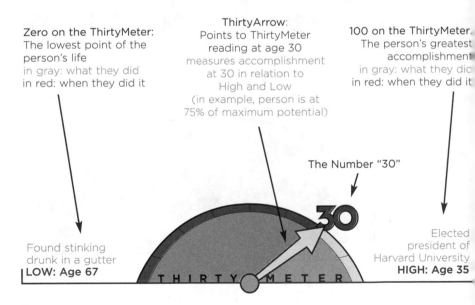

Zero on the ThirtyMeter:
The lowest point of the person's life
in gray: what they did
in red: when they did it

ThirtyArrow:
Points to ThirtyMeter reading at age 30
measures accomplishment at 30 in relation to High and Low
(in example, person is at 75% of maximum potential)

100 on the ThirtyMeter:
The person's greatest accomplishment
in gray: what they did
in red: when they did it

The Number "30"

Found stinking drunk in a gutter
LOW: Age 67

Elected president of Harvard University
HIGH: Age 35

THIRTY METER

OMITTED DATA

Data: By 30, David Goldhaber-Gordon of Stanford University had won the inaugural George E. Valley Prize "for the discovery and elucidation of the physics of the Kondo Effect in Single Electron Transistors." In addition to studying quantum phenomena in mesoscopic semiconductor structures, David also enjoys nanoelectronics.
Reason Omitted: Funny only to certain particle physicists.

Data: Pattycake turned 30 on Sept 2, 2002, at the Bronx Zoo.
Reason Omitted: Gorilla.

Data: According to his personal website, MartinReddy.net, when Martin Reddy turned 30 he had four birthday dinners and celebrated for two damn weeks.
Reason Omitted: Who the hell is Martin Reddy?

CHAPTER QUIZ

1. Which one of these people invented the phonograph?
a. Bob Dylan
b. Ted Turner
c. Pat Benatar
d. Other

2. TRUE OR FALSE?
Back betty, black bready, blam de lam!

3. ESSAY QUESTION
You are not included in this chapter. Why do you think this is? Write your own ThirtyMeter bio, examining in detail the ways in which your life went wrong (photo optional). ThirtyMeter bios should be emailed to 30@bookofages.com. Best results will be featured in *Book of Ages: Ordinary Folks.*

Alternate question: You are featured in this chapter. Hi!

Turned 30: 9/18/1991
Profession: Actor, Godfather
Place of birth: Westwood, N.J. ("I come from a nice Italian family from New Jersey.")

GANDOLFINI GOT MADE

AT 30: With stints as a bouncer and nightclub manager under his belt, James Gandolfini had realized his home was on the stage. Others were slow to realize it, so he worked odd jobs to fund his theater jones. His first paid acting gig came later that year when he was cast in a revival of *A Streetcar Named Desire.* The role led to film work. At 37, he debuted as Tony Soprano in a new HBO series about a Prozac-popping mob boss from Jersey.

> "I'd never been around actors before, and I said to myself, 'These people are nuts; this is kind of interesting.'"
> —*Gandolfini, on his first experience with acting*

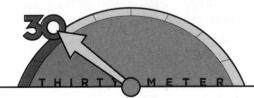

Truck driver for Gimme Seltzer delivery service
LOW: c. Age 25

THIRTY METER

Wins Emmy for Leading Actor in a Drama Series
HIGH: Age 39

Turned 30: 4/3/1954
Profession: Godfather, actor
Place of birth: Omaha, Nebraska

BRANDO ORDERED A HIT

AT 30: Seven years after his breakthrough stage turn in *A Streetcar Named Desire*, Marlon Brando starred as a washed-up boxer in *On the Waterfront*, a role that won him the Academy Award for Best Actor. As his acting reputation grew, so did his reputation as a Hollywood rebel. When he won the award for the second time nearly two decades later, for his performance in *The Godfather*, he sent Sacheen Littlefeather, a B-list actress posing as a Native American activist, to tell the Academy he refused to accept the award.

"I am sick to death of being thought of as a blue-jeaned slobber-mouth and I am sick to death of having people come up and say hello and then just stand there expecting you to throw a raccoon at them."
—*Brando, age 30*

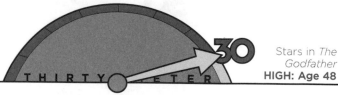

Kisses Larry King on the mouth
LOW: Age 70

THIRTY METER

Stars in *The Godfather*
HIGH: Age 48

Turned 30: 1/7/1987
Profession: Chipper morning-show anchor
Wacky sidekick: Al Roker

COURIC LIVED FOR TODAY

AT 30: Katie Couric was watching NBC's *Today Show* from afar. After working for seven years at various TV stations, she'd taken a job as a reporter at NBC's D.C. affiliate. At 32, Couric was hired to cover the Pentagon for NBC News and began filing reports for *Today*. When Couric was 34, *Today* co-host Deborah Norville took maternity leave and Couric came to the couch as her fill-in. The show's lagging ratings immediately spiked. Couric took the credit. Norville took a permanent vacation.

Frowns
(unconfirmed)
LOW: Age 17

Signs $65 million, 4.5 year deal with NBC
HIGH: Age 44

THIRTY METER

Turned 30: 8/15/1942
Profession: Julienner
Favorite ingredient: Butter

CHILD LIVED AND LET DIE

AT 30: Julia Child didn't have anything cooking, beyond a fledgling career in espionage. Working as a research assistant for the Office of Strategy Services, she went on assignment in Ceylon (now Sri Lanka) and China, where she helped the U.S. government pass secret documents to its intelligence officers. Six years later in Paris, Child attended the Le Cordon Bleu cooking school. She subsequently co-founded L'Ecole des Trois Gourmandes cooking school. Zee rest ees history.

Burns chicken as cooking-school student (unconfirmed)
LOW: Age 37

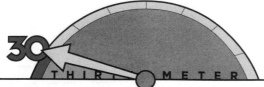

Co-authors
Mastering the Art of French Cooking
HIGH: Age 49

Turned 30: 12/12/1893
Profession: Depressionist painter
Hobbies: Travel, excessive drinking

MUNCH SCREAMED

AT 30: Edvard Munch painted his most famous work, *The Scream*. In his diary, Munch noted a moment on a bridge in Norway that served as his inspiration for the painting: "My friends walked on. I stood there, trembling with fright. And I felt a loud, unending scream piercing nature." Munch was a founder of the expressionist movement in 20th-century art. *The Scream* was one of a group of paintings that made up his emotional "Frieze of Life" series. (The paintings *Waaaa, I'm Sad* and *Damn This Crappy Brush* were abandoned.)

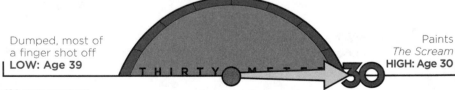

Dumped, most of
a finger shot off
LOW: Age 39

Paints
The Scream
HIGH: Age 30

Turned 30: 12/16/1800
Profession: Ivory tickler
1st published work (age 12): 9 Variations, in C Minor, for Piano

BEETHOVEN COULDN'T HEAR IT

AT 30: Ludwig van Beethoven continued to go deaf, though he would not acknowledge the full extent of the problem for a few years. By 30, he had written the *Pathétique*, three piano concertos, two symphonies, and a set of six string quartets. His musical style was beginning its transition from the high classical style to a romantic one. Much of the work for which he is best remembered lay ahead—as did total deafness and utter despair. How's that for a romantic style?

"My hearing has grown steadily worse over the last three years, which was said to be caused by the condition of my belly."
—*Beethoven, age 30, in a letter*

Forgets to mail letter to his "immortal beloved"
LOW: Age 41

THIRTYMETER

Completes Ninth Symphony
HIGH: Age 53

Turned 30: 2/11/1877
Profession: A/V club founder
Marital woe: "My wife, dearly beloved, cannot invent worth a damn!!"

EDISON | SAW THE LIGHT

AT 30: Thomas Edison changed the world—for the first time. Working to perfect the telephone transmitter, he was tinkering around with tinfoil when it occurred to him that sound could be recorded on a rapidly moving surface. He assembled a crude instrument and spoke "Mary had a little lamb" into a mouthpiece. Lo and behold, the device played the verse back to him—the world's first recorded sound. Never one to sit around, Edison upped the ante at age 31, inventing the electric lightbulb.

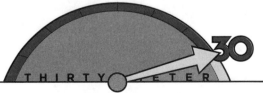

Gives up on
motion pictures
with sound
LOW: Age 68

THIRTY METER

Invents
lightbulb
HIGH: Age 31

Turned 30: 5/20/1976
Profession: Gay icon
Real name: Cherilyn Sarkisian LaPierre

CHER SOAKED UP THE SONNY

AT 30: Cher had reconciled with Sonny—sort of. With their divorce papers freshly signed and *The Sonny and Cher Comedy Hour* two years gone, the duo abandoned their solo projects and reunited for *The Sonny and Cher Show.* The reunion was strictly professional. In fact, Cher was pregnant with new husband Gregg Allman's baby. The show lasted less than two seasons, about as long as the marriage with Allman. But Cher, God bless her, had only just begun.

Dress missing one sequin (unconfirmed)
LOW: Age 28

Wins Best Actress Oscar for *Moonstruck*
HIGH: Age 41

Turned 30: 1934 (exact birthdate a corporate secret of Mars, Inc.)
Profession: Sugar daddy
Other notable creations: Uncle Ben's Converted Rice, Kal Kan & Pedigree Pet Food

MARS LIKED THE GREEN ONES

AT 30: His father struck candy-bar gold with the creation of Milky Way and Snickers in the 1920s, but Forrest Mars Sr. wanted more. By 30, he had distanced himself from his family firm and decamped to Britain, where he was manufacturing chocolate for European tastes. Soon after, Mars visited Spain and saw soldiers in the Spanish Civil War eating chocolates encased in a hard coating to stop them from melting. That inspired his creation of M&M chocolate candies, which debuted in 1941 to wide acclaim—and no sticky fingers.

> "I told my father to stick his business up his ass. I wanted to conquer the whole goddamned world."
> —*Forrest Mars Sr.*

Splits with father, heads abroad to England
LOW: Age 28

THIRTY METER

Makes M&Ms
HIGH: Age 37

Turned 30: 10/17/2002
Profession: Mack daddy
Bitches smacked (metaphorically): 124

EMINEM RAKED IN THE GREEN

"So let me just revel and bask, in the fact that I got everyone kissing my ass."
—Eminem, "Without Me"

AT 30: Three weeks after his 30th birthday, Eminem's first movie, *8 Mile,* opened. The film grossed $54.5 million its opening weekend, doubling studio expectations and establishing the controversial rapper as a box-office draw. Two months later, his album *The Eminem Show* was named the top-selling album of the year, with self-analytic lyrics like "Full of controversy, until I retire my jersey, 'til the fire inside dies and expires at thirty."

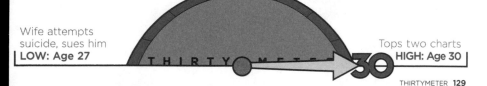

Wife attempts suicide, sues him
LOW: Age 27

Tops two charts
HIGH: Age 30

THIRTY · METER

Turned 30: 11/19/1968
Profession: Media mogul
Length of marriage to Fonda: 9 years, 5 months

TURNER | SPREAD THE NEWS

AT 30: Six years after his father's suicide, Ted Turner was working day and night to propel his family's Atlanta billboard business into the black. At 31, Turner took the profits from that business and bought a small, struggling Atlanta UHF television station. After rescuing Channel 17 from the ratings basement, he relaunched it as WTBS (Turner Broadcasting System), the first satellite superstation. The "Mouth of the South" finally had a megaphone.

Caught with co-ed in dorm room at Brown, expelled
LOW: Age 21

THIRTY METER

Named *Time* Man of the Year for CNN's coverage of Gulf War
HIGH: Age 53

Turned 30: 12/21/1967
Profession: Aerobics instructor
Length of marriage to Turner: 9 years, 5 months

"I was terrified when I turned 30. I was pregnant and had the mumps and Faye Dunaway was just coming out in *Bonnie and Clyde*. I thought, 'Oh my God, I'll never work again. I'm old!'"

—*Fonda*

FONDA SAVED THE WORLD

AT 30: Jane Fonda played the scantily clad titular hero in the 1968 film *Barbarella.* In the movie, it's the year 40,000 A.D. and an evil scientist, Duran Duran, is bent on wreaking havoc. Barbarella must save the day. Two years later, Fonda ditched the catsuit and received her first of six Best Actress Oscar nominations.

Launches national aerobics movement
LOW: Age 45

Wins first Best Actress Oscar for *Klute*
HIGH: Age 34

THIRTYMETER **131**

Turned 30: 7/12/1847
Profession: Woodsman
Family business: Lead-pencil manufacturing

THOREAU FOUND WALDO

AT 30: Henry David Thoreau left his hand-hewn home after more than two years of living life on the shores of Walden Pond. He moved into the home of Ralph Waldo Emerson in downtown Concord, Massachusetts, then, later, back to his parents' pad.

"I have lived some thirty years on this planet, and I have yet to hear the first syllable of valuable or even earnest advice from my seniors. They have told me nothing, and probably cannot tell me anything, to the purpose."

—*Thoreau,* Walden

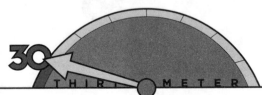

Rejects nature while climbing Mount Ktaadn
LOW: Age 29

Walden published
HIGH: Age 37

"I have completely reached my peak maturity now and am blowing such mad poetry and literature that I'll look back years later with amazement and chagrin that I can't do it anymore."

—*Kerouac, in a letter written on his 30th birthday*

Turned 30: 3/12/1952
Profession: Beatnik
Good buddies: Allen Ginsberg, William Burroughs

KEROUAC BLEW LIKE MAD

AT 30: Jack Kerouac was in the middle of the greatest creative push of his life. He wrote *Doctor Sax* and spent most of the next few years writing more than half of his major works. Unfortunately, he spent the rest of his time opening rejection letters from editors who didn't understand his "spontaneous prose." Though he wrote his most famous work, *On the Road,* before he was 30, it sat in his rucksack unpublished until he was 35.

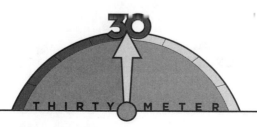

Dies from abdominal hemorrhage
LOW: Age 47

On the Road published
HIGH: Age 35

THIRTYMETER

Turned 30: 5/24/1971
Profession: Troubadour
Plugged in: 7/25/1965

DYLAN BLAM-DE-LAM'D

AT 30: "back betty, black bready, blam de lam! bloody had a bab blam de lam!" No, this wasn't Bob Dylan mumbling in concert—it was Dylan in *Tarantula*, a book published when he was 30. A year after releasing the albums *New Morning* and the widely panned *Self Portrait,* Dylan's critics speculated (with apparent justification) that he was washed up. Three years later, he proved that he wasn't all wet after all, releasing the critically successful album *Planet Waves* and, the next year, *Blood on the Tracks.*

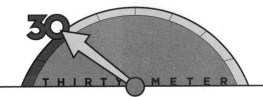

Motorcycle
accident forces
two-year hiatus
LOW: Age 25

Releases
*Blonde on
Blonde*
HIGH: Age 24

THIRTY METER

Turned 30: 10/13/1971
Profession: Balladeer
Height: 5'3"

SIMON BURNED BRIDGES

AT 30: Having just split with longtime partner Art Garfunkel after releasing *Bridge Over Troubled Water*, which sold seven million copies, Paul Simon released his first solo album three months after he turned 30. The album, cleverly titled *Paul Simon,* didn't come close to the success the duo had enjoyed, selling a mere million copies. Still, he fared better than Garfunkel, who turned 30 a month after Simon. The curly-haired one had just hit the big screen in Mike Nichols's odd paean to sexual dysfunction, *Carnal Knowledge.*

The Capeman flops on Broadway
LOW: Age 56

THIRTY○METER

Graceland wins Album of the Year Grammy
HIGH: Age 45

ROCKERS RECORDED
in the studio at age 30

ELVIS PRESLEY
Turned 30: 1/8/1965
HARUM SCARUM SOUNDTRACK

At 30, Elvis was stuck in a rut, but that didn't stop him from churning it out. The King split his time between the recording studio and the movie set, shaking his hips in *Harum Scarum, Tickle Me,* and *Girl Happy*.

TINA TURNER
Turned 30: 11/26/1968
COME TOGETHER (WITH IKE)

Whenever she was awake, and maybe when she wasn't, 30-year-old Turner was in the studio with her husband, Ike. The prolific duo released a whopping eight albums in 1969. Despite the market oversaturation, half of the albums managed to crack the charts.

JOHN LENNON
Turned 30: 10/9/1970
IMAGINE

The Beatles broke up before any of them turned 30, so Lennon had gone solo by the time he hit the three-decade mark. That year, he recorded the album *Imagine* over a three-month span in his home studio in Ascot, England. Released a few months later, it immediately shot to No. 1.

BRUCE SPRINGSTEEN
Turned 30: 9/23/1979

THE RIVER

Five years after he'd released *Born to Run,* and graced the cover of both *Time* and *Newsweek* in the same week, the Boss finally topped the charts with his fifth album, *The River*. The album also featured his first top-ten track, "Hungry Heart."

PAT BENATAR
Turned 30: 1/10/1983

LIVE FROM EARTH

After training as an opera singer, Benatar found pop-chart success by her 30th birthday and was poised to cash in with a live album. Though the album, *Live from Earth,* featured classics including "Hit Me With Your Best Shot," one of the album's two bonus studio tracks—"Love Is a Battlefield"—became a bona fide hit in its own right, hitting No. 5 on the *Billboard* charts.

BONO
Turned 30: 5/10/1990

ACHTUNG BABY

After nearly three years of touring following the release of *The Joshua Tree,* U2 returned to the studio when Bono was 30 to record a new album. Nobody could agree on how to proceed. There was a lot of yelling. Brian Eno was called in to restore order, and soon after, *Achtung Baby* hit stores to critical and popular acclaim.

Turned 30: 4/23/1594 (uncertain)
Profession: Bard
Correct pronunciation: "SHAKES-pîer"

SHAKESPEARE WENT GLOBAL

AT 30: Having left the theater world for several years to work on his poetry, William Shakespeare returned to the theater as a founding member of the theater troupe Lord Chamberlain's Men. By that time, he had written eleven plays, including *Richard III* and *The Comedy of Errors,* and had gained a valuable sponsor in the Earl of Southampton. Also at 30, Shakespeare showed off his softer side, publishing the play *Titus Andronicus,* in which two sons are killed and baked in a pie.

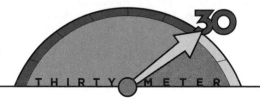

Suffers copyright breach (sonnets published without his permission)
LOW: Age 45

Pens *Hamlet*
HIGH: Age 36

THIRTY METER

Turned 30: 7/31/1995
Profession: Children's-book writer
Correct pronunciation: "ROLL-ing"

ROWLING GOT ROLLING

AT 30: On a long train ride in her mid-20s, J. K. Rowling came up with the idea for a story about a boy wizard who lives a normal life, unaware of his own powers. A single mother at 30, she was forging ahead with the character, now named Harry Potter, stealing seconds of writing time in coffee shops while her daughter slept in a carriage nearby. The book, *Harry Potter and the Sorcerer's Stone,* would be published just before Rowling turned 32, propelling her to fame, fortune, and a baby-sitter.

"It was only during the final year of writing that I found myself poorer than I'd ever been before. Obviously, continuing to write was a bit of a logistical problem."

—*Rowling*

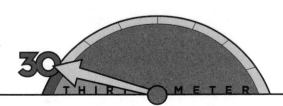

Fails to find publisher for first story, "Rabbit"
LOW: Age 6

Holds top three spots on *New York Times* best-seller list
HIGH: Age 34

Turned 30: 1/21/1970
Profession: Clubber
Nicknames: Golden Bear, Fat Jack

NICKLAUS RULED THE LINKS

AT 30: Jack Nicklaus proved you can have a belly *and* be a star athlete. By 30 he'd claimed the title of "Best Golfer in the World" and was well on his way to "Best Golfer Ever." (Tiger Woods was still just a glimmer.) Halfway through a stretch of 17 years in which he won at least one tournament each year, Nicklaus won the British Open at the three-decade mark. The Golden Bear went on to win 10 more professional majors during his career. His total of 18 is the most in golf history.

Doesn't win any
tournaments
LOW: Age 39

Finishes in
the top 10 in
82% of tour
events
HIGH: Age 31–33

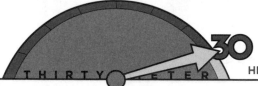

Turned 30: 11/22/1973
Profession: Racqueteer
Favorite Album: *Thriller* (unconfirmed)

KING | REIGNED ON CLAY

AT 30: A year after striking a blow for female athletes everywhere, Billie Jean King reigned as the queen at the U.S. Open for the fourth time. It was the 11th of her 12 Grand Slam tennis titles. That same year, she became the first female coach of a professional sports team that included male players. Her male charges evidently showed no ill will about the drubbing she'd administered at age 29 to 55-year-old ex-Wimbledon champ Bobby Riggs in the "Battle of the Sexes."

Sued for "galimony" by ex-lover Marilyn Barnett while married to Larry King
LOW: Age 37

THIRTY METER

Wins three grand slams
HIGH: Age 29

Turned 30: 6/12/1954
Profession: Oilman, 41st president
Nickname: Poppy

BUSH SR.　DUG FOR OIL

AT 30: George H. W. Bush was practicing being president—of the oil company Zapata Offshore. But even as he was busy drilling for Texas tea, the seeds of political dynasty were taking root around him. His father, Prescott, had moved from investment banking to the Senate, and his young sons, eight-year-old George W. and one-year-old Jeb, were wreaking havoc on the playground.

"Your Christmas presents were the hit of the day. My suit case is just perfect, Jebby never took his eyes off the record player, and George was most enthusiastic over his German cars."

—Bush Sr,
thank-you note
written at 30

Not re-elected president
LOW: Age 68

THIRTY METER

Elected president
HIGH: Age 64

Turned 30: 8/4/1931
Profession: Legendary trumpeter
Lesser-known nickname: Pops

ARMSTRONG | DUG IT

AT 30: Louis Armstrong first recorded "When It's Sleepy Time Down South," which would become his theme song. Already a star in New York and Chicago, Armstrong was creating some of the most innovative music of his career. His tour of England later that year would result in his moniker "Satchmo," a London music magazine's shortening of an earlier nickname, "Satchel Mouth." Playing for King George V, he said, "This one's for you, Rex: I'll be glad when you're dead, you rascal you."

Arrested for shooting off pistol on New Years Eve, sent to live in waif's home
LOW: Age 11

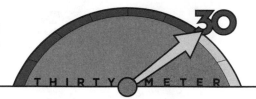

Lights up New York, makes Hollywood debut in *Pennies from Heaven*
HIGH: Age 35

THIRTYMETER

Turned 30: 8/14/1998
Profession: Hot
Named after: A department store

BERRY   WAS NO FOOL

AT 30: On the heels of a critically acclaimed performance in *Bulworth,* Halle Berry had established herself as a seven-figure actress. That year, she returned to the screen in the music biopic *Why Do Fools Fall in Love?* Soon after, she reportedly accepted a bonus payment of $500,000 for baring her breasts to John Travolta in *Swordfish*. Good move. She won a Best Actress Oscar for her very next movie, *Monster's Ball*.

Plays "Sharon Stone" in *The Flintstones*
LOW: Age 25

First African-American woman to win Best Actress Academy Award
HIGH: Age 33

Turned 30: 4/14/2003
Profession: Pianist
Childhood hobby: Breakdancing

BRODY | FELT BERRY GOOD

AT 30: Adrien Brody was still wiping Halle Berry's lipstick off of his face. Three weeks earlier, Brody had become the youngest man to win the Best Actor Academy Award—besting Richard Dreyfuss, who won it at age 30 in 1977 —and tongued his Oscar presenter, Berry, on stage. Brody was back on the big screen in short order, but he was also in the recording studio, chasing a side career as a hip-hop producer. "I told Adrien he produces like RZA, which is a big compliment," rap impresario P. Diddy told *Rolling Stone*.

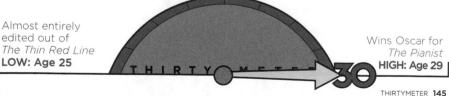

Almost entirely
edited out of
The Thin Red Line
LOW: Age 25

Wins Oscar for
The Pianist
HIGH: Age 29

THIRTYMETER

Turned 30: 1/17/1736
Profession: Kite-flying nutcase, father of democracy
Lesser-known nickname: Harmonious Human Multitude

FRANKLIN   PUT OUT

AT 30: For Ben Franklin, life wasn't all about the Benjamins. Sure, he was already a successful publisher—he'd founded the *Pennsylvania Gazette* and written *Poor Richard's Almanac*—but he was also displaying a little brotherly love. Inspired by the refined firefighting methods he'd witnessed during a trip to Boston, Franklin created Philadelphia's Union Fire Company after penning an anonymous letter to his own newspaper, urging, "An ounce of prevention is worth a pound of cure."

"At 20 years of age the will reigns, at 30 the wit, and at 40 the judgement."
—*Franklin*

Runs away from home, walks across New Jersey
LOW: Age 17

Flies his kite
HIGH: Age 46

THIRTY O METER

Turned 30: 7/24/1927
Profession: Aviatrix
Other profession: Fashion designer

EARHART | GOT IT UP

AT 30: Amelia Earhart became the first woman to complete a trans-Atlantic flight. Earhart and her flight team "Bill" Stutz and "Slim" Gordon took off one day from Newfoundland and landed 20 hours later in Wales. (Since it was an international flight, drinks were free.) Upon returning to the States, the trio was treated to a ticker-tape parade. Earhart later became the first woman to make a solo trans-Atlantic flight. She disappeared in the Pacific during an attempt to fly around the world at 39.

Crash, disappearance
LOW: Age 39

THIRTY METER

Completes trans-Atlantic flight
HIGH: Age 30

"There is a difference between twenty-nine and thirty.
When you are twenty-nine it can be the beginning of everything.
When you are thirty it can be the end of everything."

—*Gertrude Stein*

LIFE ENDS AT 30

No sense running from the truth: bodies fade, responsibilities grow, hairlines recede. But sit up straight and wipe away the tears.

In a 1972 book, Mortimer J. Adler and Charles Van Doren offered this thought on the post-30 decline: "There is a strange fact about the human mind, a fact that differentiates the mind sharply from the body. The body is limited in ways that the mind is not. One sign of this is that the body does not continue indefinitely to grow in strength and develop in skill and grace. By the time most people are thirty years old, their bodies are as good as they will ever be; in fact, many persons' bodies have begun to deteriorate by that time. But there is no limit to the amount of growth and development that the mind can sustain."

MOST SHOCKING REVELATION
Will Ferrell's movie career began in 1972 (p. 162).

LEAST SHOCKING REVELATION
Rock stars die young (p. 158).

TWO ADDITIONAL FUN FACTS ABOUT ORSON WELLES (p. 161)
1. The network wanted him as the lead on *Fantasy Island,* but Aaron Spelling insisted on Ricardo Montalban.

2. Declined an offer to be the voice of Darth Vader.

DATA OMITTED

Data: Quote from Honoré de Balzac's *A Woman of Thirty:* "Nothing is so discreet as a young face, for nothing is less mobile; it has the serenity, the surface smoothness, and the freshness of a lake. There is no character in women's faces before the age of thirty."
Reason Omitted: Read it wrong the first time; apparently complimentary.

Data: Listing of Jim Brown's profession as "fotbailer."
Reason Omitted: Egregious spelling error.

Data: Quote from Finley Peter Dunne: "If ye live enough befure thirty, ye won't care to live at all afther fifty."
Reason Omitted: "Befure" is not a word.

CHAPTER QUIZ

1. Which of the following peaked five years ago?
a. Lung capacity
b. Oxygen intake
c. Ability to exercise
d. Orson Welles's career

2. TRUE OR FALSE?
Elephants won the Battle of the Jhelum.

3. ESSAY QUESTION
Reminisce about the oldest ox you have known.

YOUR BEST YEARS ARE  BEHIND YOU · · · · · · · · · · ·

At 30, your body begins a slow fade to the grave

· **BONE DENSITY** Now **thinning** up to **10%** **per decade**

· **STAMINA** Decreased by **one minute** from your 20s

· **MUSCLE MASS** **Down 10% per decade,** starting now

· **LUNG CAPACITY** Peaked **five years ago**

· **OXYGEN INTAKE** Down **1%** **per year,** starting now

· **FLEXIBILITY** You can still **touch your toes...**
but by 40, you'll be lucky to reach your shins

"THE FACES OF MOST AMERICAN WOMEN OVER THIRTY ARE RELIEF MAPS OF PETULANT AND BEWILDERED UNHAPPINESS."

—*F. Scott Fitzgerald, letter to his daughter*

Under-35s account for **28%** of all cosmetic surgery

Women account for **89%** of all cosmetic surgery

By age 30 **25%** of men begin to show baldness

"THIRTY—THE PROMISE OF A DECADE OF LONELINESS, A THINNING LIST OF SINGLE MEN TO KNOW, A THINNING BRIEFCASE OF ENTHUSIASM, THINNING HAIR."

—*F. Scott Fitzgerald,* The Great Gatsby
(published when Fitzgerald was 28)

PAGING MR. REAPER! MOST COMMON WAYS TO DIE · · · · ·

at age 30

29% ACCIDENTS

12% SUICIDE

10% HOMICIDE

10% CANCER

7% HEART DISEASE

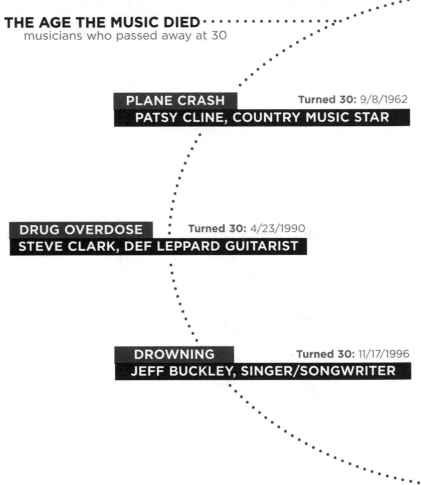

THE AGE THE MUSIC DIED
musicians who passed away at 30

PLANE CRASH
Turned 30: 9/8/1962
PATSY CLINE, COUNTRY MUSIC STAR

DRUG OVERDOSE
Turned 30: 4/23/1990
STEVE CLARK, DEF LEPPARD GUITARIST

DROWNING
Turned 30: 11/17/1996
JEFF BUCKLEY, SINGER/SONGWRITER

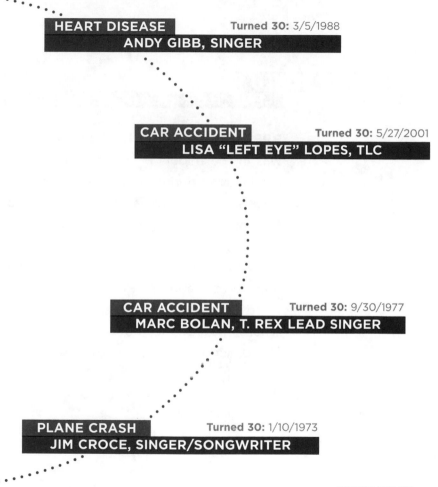

HEART DISEASE   **Turned 30:** 3/5/1988
ANDY GIBB, SINGER

CAR ACCIDENT   **Turned 30:** 5/27/2001
LISA "LEFT EYE" LOPES, TLC

CAR ACCIDENT   **Turned 30:** 9/30/1977
MARC BOLAN, T. REX LEAD SINGER

PLANE CRASH   **Turned 30:** 1/10/1973
JIM CROCE, SINGER/SONGWRITER

Turned 30: 10/27/1962
Profession: Depressive poet
Pseudonym used for _The Bell Jar_: Victoria Lucas

SYLVIA PLATH
PUT HER HEAD IN THE OVEN

BREAKTHROUGH: On her 30th birthday, Plath was in the middle of a two-month period of productivity during which she wrote the forty poems "of rage, despair, love, and vengeance" for which she is best remembered.

BREAKDOWN: On that same birthday, Plath and her husband, Ted Hughes, had been separated for a few weeks. She moved to London, where she saw her novel _The Bell Jar_ published, and gassed herself to death.

Her dead
Body wears the smile of accomplishment.
        —_Lines from Plath's final poem,
        written a week before her suicide_

Turned 30: 5/6/1945
Profession: Hearst-baiter
Most hot dogs eaten in one sitting: 18

ORSON WELLES
WAS ON THE ROAD TO XANADU

BREAKTHROUGH: Five years before he turned 30, Welles was king of the hill. He debuted on Broadway at 19, was a radio star with *War of the Worlds* at 23, and had just landed a multiple-movie contract with RKO.

BREAKDOWN: By 30, Welles's sled was careening downhill. *Citizen Kane* had been lambasted by critics, tanked at the box office, and was booed at the Oscars. His next movies fared no better. At 33, Welles exiled himself to Europe. Though he continued to work as an actor and director for the rest of his life, he never lived up to the promise of his youth.

LOGAN'S RUN

"The only thing you can't have in this perfect world of total pleasure is your 30th birthday... Logan is 29."
—*Tagline for* Logan's Run

In 2274, survivors of a holocaust live in a domed city near Washington, D.C. The computers that run the city have decided that, in order to to keep the population down, inhabitants can live only until they turn 30. Logan (Michael York) is a "Sandman" who must hunt down people trying to escape. But he decides 30 isn't so bad, and sets out to destroy the system. Peter Ustinov and Farrah Fawcett-Majors also star. (MGM, 1976)

THE AVERAGE
AGE OF RETIREMENT
FOR NFL PLAYERS:

30

Turned 30: 2/17/1966
Profession: Bruiser
Hobbies: Founder, Cleveland Browns, Brown University (unconfirmed)

JIM BROWN
GAVE THE NFL THE SHAFT

BREAKTHROUGH: By the time Jim Brown retired from the NFL at 30, he had led the league in rushing eight times and held career marks for yards rushing, yards per carry, and touchdowns. Many considered him the greatest football player of all time.

BREAKDOWN: When Brown left football, he turned to acting—bad acting. He appeared in over 30 films, including *Slaughter* (tagline: "It's not only his name it's his business and sometimes—his pleasure!") and *Slaughter's Big Rip-Off* (tagline: "The mob put the finger on Slaughter... so he gave them the finger right back—curled tight around a trigger!").

Turned 30: 326 B.C.
Profession: Great
Failed professions: Wonderful, tall, handsome, terrific, kind-hearted, timid

ALEXANDER THE GREAT
GOT GREECED UP

BREAKTHROUGH: Having conquered Persia to rule an empire stretching from the Mediterranean to Afghanistan, the Great wanted more. He marched his army from Greece to India. After facing enormous battle elephants for the first time, his army won its last significant fight, the Battle of the Jhelum.

BREAKDOWN: At 33, he died, likely of malaria.

HIS HORSE AT 30: Buceph'alos, Alexander's beloved horse, died at 30. Alexander built a city, called Buceph'ala, for the horse's remains. The name Buceph'alos means "ox-head." · · Alexander's dog was named "cat-ass."*

*unconfirmed

At the age of 30, the **THIRTY YEARS WAR** was over

The **AVERAGE OX** lives 30 years

Conclusion:
It is possible, but unlikely, that
some ox took part in the
entire Thirty Years War

REDEMPTION SONG

climbing back on top after 30

STEVE JOBS
Turned 30: 2/24/1985

THOUGHT APPLE WAS ROTTEN

At 30, Jobs resigned in a huff from Apple Computer, the company he'd co-founded, after a dispute with the CEO he'd hired. He immediately formed NeXT Inc. and bought a majority stake in Pixar. In the 1990s, Pixar would find success with films like *Toy Story,* and in 1996 Jobs returned to lead Apple back to glory after the company bought NeXT for $400 million.

EDDIE MURPHY
Turned 30: 4/3/1991

WATCHED HIS CAREER BOOMERANG

Seven years after rocketing to stardom with *Beverly Hills Cop,* Murphy was filming the bland romantic comedy *Boomerang* at 30. The movie prompted *Rolling Stone* to observe, "What Murphy's doing isn't acting; it's masturbation." Murphy's career continued its downward spiral with a series of bombs until his remake of *The Nutty Professor* at 35 re-established his box-office drawing power.

MOLLY RINGWALD
Turned 30: 2/18/1998

BUSTED OUT OF DETENTION

With *Sixteen Candles,* Ringwald became a national sensation. By 30 candles, she was another child star trying to prove that she could play grown-up. After enduring a series of B-list roles, Ringwald made a splash again at 33 with a starring turn on Broadway in *Cabaret.* The *New York Times* called her "more than just the latest in a long succession of celebrity Sallies."

MICHAEL JORDAN
Turned 30: 2/17/1993
PLAYED WITH THE WRONG BALLS

When he was 30, Jordan signed a contract to play for the Birmingham Barrons, a minor-league baseball team. Earlier that year he'd led the Chicago Bulls to their third straight NBA championship—and then walked away from the game. But in his baseball rookie season, he struck out 114 times. After a season and a half of missed curveballs, Jordan laced up his high-tops and returned to the court. By 35, he had three more NBA titles.

HEATHER LOCKLEAR
Turned 30: 9/25/1991
WAS THROUGH WITH HOOKERS

After turning heads on *Dynasty* and *T.J. Hooker*, Locklear's late 20s and early 30s were dominated by TV movies like *Return of the Swamp Thing* (for which she won a worst-actress Golden Raspberry). She hit the big time again at 32, when she took up residence in *Melrose Place*. She moved to *Spin City* at 38. The two shows brought Locklear six Golden Globe nominations.

BABE RUTH
Turned 30: 2/6/1925
GOT A TUMMYACHE

He'd led the Yankees to a championship, but at 30, Ruth's appetites were catching up with him. Legend has it that in spring training Ruth suffered a stomachache. Some say he'd eaten a dozen hot dogs and consumed eight bottles of soda; others suggested he had venereal disease. When he ended up in the hospital, one newspaper declared him dead. Ruth returned to the field in June, but he wasn't the Babe of old, and the Yanks finished in seventh place. At 32, Ruth led his team back to glory as the leader of the legendary "Murderer's Row."

What are the odds you'll live to see **YOUR LATE THIRTIES?** • • •

· · · · · · · · · · · · · · Glad you asked. Exactly **99.0030%**

·

AS REGARDS "EARLY 30s" AND "30s"

Throughout this book, "early 30s" refers to ages 30–34 and "30s" refers to ages 30–39, unless otherwise noted below.

CHAPTER 1: YOU ARE 30

p. 1: Lyrics from Grace Slick, "Lather," published by Mole Music Co. (BMI). Appears on Jefferson Airplane, *Crown of Creation*, 1968.

p. 4: Quote from *The New Oxford American Dictionary*, Oxford University Press, 2001.

p. 7: Linux stat from Linux.org, which claims 31% of all Linux users are between 25 and 34, second only to users 18–24 (37%). Telemarketer stat from "Watch Your Tongue! Words and Greetings That May Offend," The Harris Poll #56, Nov. 14, 2001 (www.harrisinteractive.com); stat is ages 30–39. Results in response to the question, "When you get a sales or customer-service call from someone you don't know, would you prefer to be addressed by your first name or by your last name, or don't you care one way or the other?"

p. 9: Stats from U.S. Census 2000 (www.census.gov). Number of Americans turning 30 "this year" based on the total number of 27-year-olds in 2000 who are presumably turning 30 in 2003. The number of "Americans in their 30s" based on the total number of 27- to 36-year-olds in 2000 who are presumably turning 30–39 age group in 2003.

p. 10: Stats from U.S. Census 2000; median income stats are ages 25–34.

p. 11: Height and weight stats from workerscompensation.com.

p. 12: First stat and quote from "Work and Family: Turning Thirty—Job Mobility and Labor Market Attachment," Report 862, U.S. Department of Labor, Bureau of Labor Statistics, Dec. 1993; stat is those employed on their 30th birthday. Second stat from "Employee Tenure in 2002," U.S. Department of Labor, Bureau of Labor Statistics, Sept. 2002; stat is ages 30–34.

p. 13: First three stats and quote from "Work and Family: Turning Thirty—Job Mobility and Labor Market Attachment," Report 862, U.S. Department of Labor, Bureau of Labor Statistics, Dec. 1993; stats are those employed on their 30th birthday. Fourth stat from "Number of Jobs Held, Labor Market Activity, and Earnings Growth Over Two Decades: Results from a Longitudinal Survey," U.S. Department of Labor, Bureau of Labor Statistics, April 2000; stat is for ages 30–34.

pp. 14–15: Stats from "Number of Jobs Held, Labor Market Activity, and Earnings Growth Over Two Decades: Results from a Longitudinal Survey," U.S. Department of Labor, Bureau of Labor Statistics, April 2000. Stats on p. 14 are employed individuals ages 30–34 who were promoted between 1995 and 1997. Stats on p. 15 are ages 30–34.

pp. 16–17: Here's the math. Seven dog years equals one human year—source: popular wisdom. Planetary years measure complete revolutions around the sun—source: NASA. February 29 only comes around once every four years—source: handy desk calendar. Quote from Gertrude Stein, *Everybody's Autobiography*, Ch. 4, Random House, 1937.

p. 18: Stats from Edward O. Laumann, John H. Gagnon, Robert T. Michael, and Stuart Michaels, *The Social Organization of Sexuality: Sexual Practices in the United States*, The University of Chicago Press, 2000, p. 356.

p. 20: Men's fitness stats from Adam Campbell, "A Fit Man Can...," *Men's Health* (www.menshealth.com). Women's fitness stats from "Shape Your Best Life Fitness Tests," *Shape* (www.shape.com), April 2002. Stats are for 30-year-olds; run stats in minutes. The "1.5 Mile Run" is described in *Shape* as "1.5 Mile Walk/Run Cardio Test," with, alas, no clarification offered to determine what that is. Quote from "Health Tips: Snow Shoveling Can Be Life-Threatening," Ohio Dept. of Health, Oct. 2000.

p. 21: First two stats from "Smoking, Obesity, and Not Using Seat Belts Much More Common Among People with the Least Education," The Harris Poll #15, Mar. 3, 1999. Third stat from National Health and Nutrition Examination Survey, CDC, 1994. Quote from Council on Size & Weight Discrimination (www.cswd.org).

p. 22: Alcohol and illicit drugs stats from "2001 National Survey on Substance Abuse," Substance Abuse and Mental Health Services Administration (www.samhsa.gov). Cigarettes stat from Harris Poll #15, Mar. 3, 1999.

p. 23: For information on this 30-year-old Scotch, visit www.unusualwhiskey.com.

p. 24: Quote from Constance J. Jones and William Meredith, "Developmental Paths of Psychological Health From Early Adolescence to Later Adulthood," *Psychology and Aging,* Vol. 15, No. 2, 2000. Authors' take on Rorschach inkblot test—Albertson: "Buddha with sheep"; Steele: "poodles on parade"; Van Gieson: "cheese."

p. 25: Stats from Laumann et al., *The Social Organization of Sexuality: Sexual Practices in the United States,* The University of Chicago Press, 2000. Quote from Schizophrenia.com.

p. 27: Stats from "Gun Ownership: Two in Five Americans Live in Gun-Owning Households," The Harris Poll #25, May 30, 2001. Results in response to the question, "Do you happen to have in your home or garage any guns or revolvers?" If yes, "Do you have a pistol or not?" "Do you have a shotgun or not?" "Do you have a rifle or not?"

p. 28: Stats from "Huge Differences Between Values of Young Adults and Older Adults," The Harris Poll #58, Oct. 4, 2000; stats for "people in their 20s" are ages 25–29. Results in response to the question, "People have different ideas about what's right and wrong. As I read things some people do, tell me whether you think each one is absolutely wrong under all circumstances, wrong under most but not all circumstances, wrong only sometimes, or not wrong at all."

p. 29: NASCAR stats from "Almost Half of All Adults Watch NASCAR Races," The Harris Poll #17, March 17, 1999; stats for "people in their 20s" is ages 25–29. Results in response to the question, "About how many times in the last year have you watched a NASCAR race on TV?" Yosemite stat from self-identified respondents to a poll on the official Yosemite website (www.yosemite.ca.us), Feb. 2003. Results in response to the question, "I was how old when I first visited Yosemite?" New Year's stats from Marist College Institute for Public Opinion poll, 1995; stats are "30 years old and over." Results in response to the questions, "Are you very likely, somewhat likely, or not likely at all to make a New Year's resolution?" and "If you made a resolution last year, did you keep it?" Results are for those who answered "very likely" or "somewhat likely" (39% of over-30s said they were very/somewhat likely, versus 65% of under-30s; 66% of over-30s said they kept their resolution last year, versus 40% of under-30s.) Quote from William James, *Principles of Psychology,* Vol. 1, Ch. 4, 1890.

p. 31: Stats from respondents to a poll on Queer Astrology (www.gay-astrology.com), Feb. 2003. Results in response to the questions, "How old were you when you first realized you were gay/lesbian/TG?" and "How old were you when you came out of the closet?"

p. 32: Stats from "Current Population Survey," U.S. Department of Commerce, Bureau of the Census, March 1997. Comedians factoid from

"Sources for Campaign News," The Pew Research Center for People and the Press, 2001; compares ages 18–29 with ages 30–49.

p. 33: Stats from U.S. Census 2000. Quote from "Remarks as Prepared for Delivery by Vice President Al Gore," Jan. 12, 1999.

p. 34: Stats from Arthur B. Kennickell, Martha Starr-McCluer, and Brian J. Surette, "Recent Changes in U.S. Family Finances: Results from the 1998 Survey of Consumer Finances," Federal Reserve Bulletin, Jan. 2000; value is median; stat is families with head of household under 35.

p. 35: Stats from "Housing Vacancies and Homeownership Annual Statistics: 2001," U.S. Census.

CHAPTER 2: LIFE BEGINS AT 30

p. 36: Quote from Hervey Allen, *Anthony Adverse,* Ch. 31, 1933.

p. 38: Quote from Dave Herber, W8Lifter.com.

p. 39: Identity theft stat from "Identity Theft Complaint Data," Federal Trade Commission, June 2001. Tubman details from PBS Online (www.pbs.org). It is believed that Tubman was born in 1820 and that she returned to the South to free slaves for the first time in 1850, although exact dates are unknown. Grandma Moses details from "Grandma Moses Is Dead at 101," *New York Times,* Dec. 14, 1961.

p. 40: Details from The Internet Movie Database (www.imdb.com; hereafter abbreviated as "IMDb") and Yahoo! Movies (movies.yahoo.com).

p. 42: Details from E! Online (www.eonline. com), AllStarz.org, and IMDb. Quote from E! Online.

p. 43: Quote at top and details from Luke 3:23, *The Holy Bible.* Quote concerning Jesus' age

from Phil Stone's Bible Time (www.bibletime.com).

pp. 44–45: Rule of 100 details from Ameritrade Education Center (www. ameritrade.com). Ten percent rate of return stats from SmartMoney.com.

p. 46: Details from Oprah.com and CNN.com. Premiere show guest was the guest on Oprah's first nationally syndicated show in 1986. The company names are even better when one considers that "Harpo" is "Oprah" backward.

p. 47: Details from NBC (www.nbc.com) and Yahoo! Movies. Quote from Tom Shales, "Go Gently into That Good Night Already," *Washington Post,* Oct. 1993. In point of fact, O'Brien is actually 6´4˝, says Hollywood.com.

pp. 48–49: Austen details from The Republic of Pemberly (www.pemberly.com) and BBC (www.bbc.co.uk). Alger details from HoratioAlger.com and The Horatio Alger Society (www.ihot.com/~has/). Joyce details from Zack Bowen, Ed., *The Florida James Joyce Series* (www.upf.com/se-joyce.html) and Irelandseye.com; there is some debate about whether Maunsel, the publisher, actually burned the *Dubliners* manuscript or whether Joyce merely *thought* it did. Vonnegut details from Frank Houston, "The Salon Interview: Kurt Vonnegut," Salon.com, Oct. 8, 1999 and Kurt-Vonnegut.com. Rice details from Barry Wayne Veinotte, "An In-Depth Look into Anne Rice," Empire:Zine (www.empirezine.com) and IMDb. Tan details from "Interview: Amy Tan, Best-Selling Novelist," The Academy of Achievement (www.achievement.org), June 28, 1996 and BookBrowse.com.

pp. 50–51: Details from Emerils.com, the Food Network (www.foodtv.com), IMDb, and Linda Stasi, "Emeril Lite," *New York Post,* Sept. 25, 2001. Quote from E. Cobham Brewer, *Dictionary of Phrase and Fable,* 1898.

p. 52: Details from PBS Online and Jim Zwick, Ed., "Mark Twain," BoondocksNet.com (www.boondocksnet.com/twainwww/). Quote from Albert Bigelow Paine, *Mark Twain: A Biography*, Harper & Brothers, 1912; Internet Ed., BoondocksNet.com, 2001.

p. 53: Details from Howard University, CNN.com, and Oprah.com.

pp. 54–55: Details from "Interview with Mr. T.," *The A-Team File #1*, 1983, and IMDb. Quote from *People*, Dec. 26, 1983–Jan. 2, 1984.

p. 56: Lewis details from ESPN.com and CNNSI (www.cnnsi.com). Smith details from The Baseball Almanac (www.baseball-almanac.com); quote from Steven Wine, "Marlins' Smith Shakes Off Jinx to Return as 30-year-old Rookie," Associated Press, May 8, 2001. Bellinger details from The Baseball Almanac; quote from Tara Sullivan, "For Bellinger, a Blessing a Day," *Bergen Record*, Oct. 12, 1999.

p. 57: Details and rule excerpts from the Naismith Memorial Basketball Hall of Fame (www.hoophall.com). Quote from James Naismith, "On the Origins of Basket Ball," Speech at Springfield College, 1932.

p. 59: Details from ReelInsider.com and IMDb.

CHAPTER 3: LOVE & SEX AT 30

p. 60: Quote from George Gordon Noel ("Lord") Byron, Leslie A. Marchand, Ed., *Byron's Letters and Journals Vol. 10: A Heart for Every Fate, 1822–1823*, Books on Demand, 1973; from a letter dated Jan. 18, 1823.

p. 63: Contraception stats from Joyce Abma et al., "Fertility, Family Planning, and Women's Health: New Data from the 1995 National Survey of Family Growth," CDC/National Center for Health Statistics, Series 23, No. 19, May 1997. Quote from "Marilyn Monroe, Arthur Miller Married in White Plains Court," *New York Times*, June 30, 1956.

pp. 64–65: Stats from U.S. Census, Marital Status and Living Arrangements, March 1994. Fanny Fink quote from the film *Keiner Liebt Mich*, 1994. Miranda quote from *Sex and the City*, Ep. 15, "The Freak Show," Home Box Office, June 20, 1999.

pp. 66–67: 1997 Durex Global Sex Survey (www.durex.com).

pp. 68–69: Abma et al., "Fertility, Family Planning, and Women's Health: New Data from the 1995 National Survey of Family Growth," CDC/National Center for Health Statistics, Series 23, No. 19, May 1997; stats for women 30–34. Quote from Emily Post, *Etiquette in Society, in Business, in Politics and at Home,* Funk & Wagnalls, 1922; Internet ed., Bartleby.com, 1999. For other interesting tidbits about cohabitation and such, visit Cohabitation Nation (www.cohabitation nation.com) and the Alternatives to Marriage Project (www.unmarried.org).

pp. 70–71: Details from IMDb. *The Bachelor* is a remake of Buster Keaton's *Seven Chances* (1925). In Keaton's film, Jimmie is on the clock a day shy of his 27th birthday.

pp. 72–77: Stats from James A. Davis, Peter V. Marsden, and Tom W. Smith, *General Social Survey 1972–2000*, cumulative file, 3rd version, National Opinion Research Center, Chicago, Illinois, 2001. Extracted from the data file stored at sda.berkeley.edu; stats are for ages 25–34 covering sexual activity since age 18. Stats inside circles on pp. 76-77 from Laumann et al., *The Social Organization of Sexuality: Sexual Practices in the United States*, The University of Chicago Press, 2000, p. 305.

p. 78: Quote from Wilt Chamberlain, *A View From Above*, Dutton Books, 1992. We did the math with Microsoft Excel.

p. 79: Quote from Charles Darwin, *On the Origin of Species*, 1859; Internet ed., Literature. org, 1999. We did the math with an abacus.

pp. 80–81: Stats from Rose M. Kreider and Jason M. Fields, "Number, Timing, and Duration of Marriages and Divorces: 1996," U.S. Census Bureau Current Population Reports, Feb. 2002, pp. 70–80. Quote from Hesiod, *Works and Days*, line 695; Internet ed., Online Medieval & Classical Library (sunsite.berkeley.edu), 1995.

pp. 82–83: Taylor details from Swingin' Chicks of the '60s (www.swinginchicks.com) and IMDb. Presidents details from CampVISHUS. org and AmericanPolitics.info. Madonna details from MTV (www.mtv.com), IMDb, and Amazon.com. Monroe details from "Marilyn Monroe, Arthur Miller Married in White Plains Court," *New York Times*, June 30, 1956. Kafka details from Ronald A. Hayman, *Kafka: A Biography*, Phoenix Press, 2001, p. 164, and Kafka-Franz.com. In *The Trial*, Josef K. is arrested on the morning of his 30th birthday.

pp. 84–87: Stats from Abma et al., "Fertility, Family Planning, and Women's Health: New Data from the 1995 National Survey of Family Growth," CDC/National Center for Health Statistics, Series 23, No. 19, May 1997; stats are women 30–34.

p. 89: Joyce A. Martin et al., "Births: Final Data for 2000," CDC/National Center for Health Statistics, National Vital Statistics Report, Vol. 50, No. 5, Feb. 12, 2002.

CHAPTER 4: MONEY & POWER AT 30

p. 90: Quote from BrainyQuote.com.

p. 92: Collection letter quote based on prose from SendSnailmail.com.

p. 93: Albright details from ABC News (abcnews.go.com) and the Radcliffe Institute for Advanced Studies.

pp. 94–95: Stats from the Bill Gates Net Worth Page (www.quuxuum.org/~evan/bgnw.html). Quote from Edward William Bok, *The Americanization of Edward Bok*, 1921.

pp. 96–97: Expected retirement age stats from "3.7 Million People Over 55 Not Working Now Are Ready, Willing and Able to Work," The Harris Poll #62, Mar. 17, 1999. Results in response to the question, "At what age do you expect to stop working in a paid job?" Other stats from Kennickell et al., "Recent Changes in U.S. Family Finances: Results from the 1998 Survey of Consumer Finances," Federal Reserve Bulletin, January 2000; stats for families with head of household under 35 years old; values are median.

p. 98: Stat from Bernice Kanner, *Are You Normal About Money? Do You Behave Like Everyone Else?*, Bloomberg Press, 2001.

pp. 99–101: Stats from Kennickell et al., "Recent Changes in U.S. Family Finances: Results from the 1998 Survey of Consumer Finances," Federal Reserve Bulletin, January 2000; stats are for families with head of household under 35 years old. On p. 101, values are median.

pp. 102–103: Sleep stats from "1998 Omnibus Sleep in America Poll," the National Sleep Foundation (www.sleepfoundation.org). Raise stats from "Number of Jobs Held, Labor Market Activity, and Earnings Growth Over Two Decades: Results from a Longitudinal Survey," U.S. Department of Labor, Bureau of Labor Statistics, April 2000; stats based on average annual percent growth in real hourly earnings, 1978–1998.

p. 104: Details and quote from Christopher Byron, *Martha Inc.: The Incredible Story of Martha Stewart Living Omnimedia*, John Wiley & Sons, 2002. Stock quote assumes .03% daily growth from basis price on March 16, 2003 until the minute you are reading this book.

p. 105: Details from AOL Time Warner (www.timewarner.com). Quote from Marc Gunther, "These Guys Want It All," *Fortune*, Feb. 7, 2000. Stock quote is fabricated.

p. 107: Stats from Ellen Goodman, "Shortage of Women in the Pipeline to Higher Knowledge" *Boston Globe*, Dec. 6, 2000. Quote sourced from PaulAndrews.com. This '60s catchphrase is also attributed to Jack Weinberg and, more spuriously, Bob Dylan.

p. 108: Details from WhiteHouse.gov, CNN.com, and the Presidential Pet Museum (www.presidentialpetmuseum.com).

p. 109: Details from WhiteHouse.gov and the Presidential Pet Museum. Quote from Julia Reed, "The Son Also Rises," *Weekly Standard*, Feb. 10, 1997.

pp. 110–111: McCarthy details from Thomas C. Reeves, *The Life and Times of Joe McCarthy: A Biography*, Stein and Day, 1982. Ashcroft details from PBS Online. Kennedy details from AmericanPresidents.org. Thomas details from SupremeCourtHistory.org. Dole details from CNN.com. Biden details from Senate.gov.

p. 112: Details from The Maoist Documentation Project (www.maoism.org). Quote sourced from aish.com. A variation of this quote is often attributed to Winston Churchill; authoritative authorship is impossible to determine.

p. 113: Details from ABC News and CNN.com.

pp. 114–115: Thatcher details from Paul Johnson, "Leaders & Revolutionaries: Margaret Thatcher," *Time 100*, Time.com. Wm. the Conqueror details from BBC; year of birth is uncertain, so he may have turned 30 in 1058. Napoleon details from PBS Online. Isabella details from TheHistoryNet (www.thehistorynet.com). Mandela details from ANC.org. Gorbachev details from George W. Church, "The Education of Mikhail Sergeyevich Gorbachev," *Time*, Jan. 4, 1988.

CHAPTER 5: THIRTYMETER

p. 116: Quote from Pablo Picasso, "Letter to Daniel-Henry Kahnweiler," Sept. 17, 1912, Archives Kahnweiler-Leiris via Enrique Mallen's On-Line Picasso Project (www.tamu.edu/mocl/picasso). At age 30, Picasso also wondered, "What will I do about the dog?"

p. 119: Goldhaber-Gordon details from Stanford University. Pattycake details from "Monkey Around Weekend at Zoo," *Bronx Times Reporter*, Aug. 22, 2002. Reddy details from Martin Reddy's Home Page (www.martinreddy.net).

p. 120: Details and quote from Gina Bellafonte, "Call Him a Made Man," *Time*, Mar. 22, 1999, People.com, and Gandolfini.com.

p. 121: Details from Richard Schickel, "The Actor: Marlon Brando," *Time 100*, Time.com, and E! Online. Quote from "Tiger in the Reeds," *Time*, Oct. 11, 1954.

p. 122: Details from MSNBC.com and E! Online.

p. 123: Details from StarChefs.com and Britannica Online (www.eb.com).

p. 124: Details from Bill Van Siclen, "More to Munch," *Providence Journal*, Apr. 5, 2001 and Edvard Munch—The Dance of Life Site (www.edvard-munch.com). Quote from museSpace (www.musespace.com).

p. 125: Details from Stanley Sadie, Ed., *The New Grove Concise Dictionary of Music,* W. W. Norton, 1994. Quote from LVBeethoven.com.

p. 126: Details from PBS Online and the Library of Congress (www.loc.gov). Quote from Kathleen McAuliffe, "The Undiscovered World of Thomas Edison," *Atlantic Monthly*, Dec. 1995.

p. 127: Details from Heidi Stevens, "Turning Back Time," *Chicago Tribune*, July 20, 2002, TV Tome (www.tvtome.com), and IMDb.

p. 128: Details and quote from "Candy Man Mars," *Good Bye: The Journal of Contemporary Obituaries,* July 1999, and MMs.com. In fact, his birthday really is a corporate secret.

p. 129: Details from John Zahlaway, "*The Eminem Show* crowned 2002's No. 1 album," SoundSpike News, Jan. 3, 2003, and IMDb. Lyrics from Eminem, "Without Me" and "Soldier," *The Eminem Show,* 2002.

p. 130: Details from Hollywood.com and the *Brown Daily Herald* (www.browndailyherald.com).

p. 131: Details from Hollywood.com and IMDb. Quote from Quotes on Ageing (home.vicnet. net.au/~ac99/involved/quotes.html).

p. 132: Details and quote from Henry David Thoreau, *Walden,* 1854; modern edition, H. D. Thoreau, Joseph Wood Krutch, Ed., *Walden and Other Writings,* Bantam Books, 1989, p. 111, and Biography.com. Thoreau wrote in *The Maine Woods* of his momentarily negative view of man's relationship with nature: "Vast, Titanic, inhuman Nature has got him at disadvantage, caught him alone, and pilfers him of some of his divine faculty."

p. 133: Details and quote from Ann Charters, Ed., *Jack Kerouac: Selected Letters 1940–56,* Viking, 1995, pp. 335–337.

p. 134: Details from RollingStone.com. Quote from Bob Dylan, *Tarantula,* St. Martin's, 1994.

p. 135: Details from PaulSimon.com, MTV.com, and IMDb.

pp. 136–137: Presley details from Elvis.com and the AMG All Music Guide (www.allmusic.com). Turner details from the AMG All Music Guide and www.tina-turner.com. Lennon details from the AMG All Music Guide. Springsteen details from RollingStone.com. Benatar details from 80sVideos.com and Rollingstone.com. Bono details from the AMG All Music Guide and MuchMusic.net.

p. 138: Details from G. Blakemore Evans, Ed., *The Riverside Shakespeare,* Houghton Mifflin College, 1997, and AbsoluteShakespeare.com.

p. 139: Details from CNN.com and Scholastic (www.scholastic.com). Quote from Margaret Weir, "Of Magic and Single Motherhood," Salon.com, Mar. 31, 1999.

p. 140: Details from PGA.com.

p. 141: Details from Larry Schwartz, "Billie Jean Won for All Women," ESPN.com, and the International Tennis Hall of Fame (www. tennisfame.com)

p. 142: Details from WhiteHouse.gov and the George Bush Presidential Library and Museum (bushlibrary.tamu.edu). Quote from George H. W. Bush, *All the Best, George Bush: My Life and Other Writings,* Scribner, 1999.

p. 143: Details from PBS Online and Jeff Fitzgerald, "An Evening with the Pops," AllAboutJazz.com. Quote from Stanley Crouch, "The Musician: Louis Armstrong," *Time 100,* Time.com.

p. 144: Details from IMDb and Jam! Showbiz (www.canoe.ca/Jam).

p. 145: Details from IMDb and FilmSite.org. Quote from Robert Osbourne, *70 Years of Oscar: The Official History of the Academy Awards,* Abbeville Press, 1999.

p. 146: Details from USHistory.org. Quote from Ben Franklin, *Poor Richard's Almanac,* June 1741.

p. 147: Details from Amelia Earhart Birthplace Museum (www.ameliaearhartmuseum.org) and AmeliaEarhart.com.

CHAPTER 6: LIFE ENDS AT 30

p. 148: Quote from Gertrude Stein, *Mrs. Reynolds and Five Earlier Novelettes,* Part IV, Yale University Press, 1952.

p. 150: Welles details from IMDb. Quote from Mortimer J. Adler and Charles Van Doren, *How to Read a Book: The Classic Guide to Intelligent Reading,* Simon & Schuster, 1972.

p. 151: Quotes from Honoré De Balzac, *A Woman of Thirty, The Works of Honoré de Balzac,* vol. V, trans. by George Saintsbury, 1971 and Finley Peter Dunne, *Dooley's Opinions,* "Casual Observations," 1901.

p. 153: Stats 1,3,4,6 from Edmund Burke, "Will Aging Air Jordan Still Be Able to Fly?" *USA Today,* Oct. 30, 2001. Stat 2 from Ed G. Lakatta, MD, "Are You in Shape for Your Age?" HealthandAge.com, April 7, 2000; stamina is defined by ability to stay on a treadmill. Stat 5 from OxygenForHealth.com.

p. 154: Stats from *ASAPS 2000 Statistics,* American Society for Aesthetic Plastic Surgery (www.surgery.org). Quote from F. Scott Fitzgerald letter to his daughter, Oct. 5, 1940, in Edmund Wilson, Ed., *The Crack-Up,* New Directions, 1945.

p. 155: Stat from "Hair Loss," A.D.A.M., Inc., Yahoo! Health (health.yahoo.com), July 29, 2001. Quote from F. Scott Fitzgerald, *The Great Gatsby,* Scribner's, 1925.

p. 157: Stats from "National Vital Statistics Report," Vol. 50, No. 16, CDC, Sept. 16, 2002; stats are ages 25–34.

pp. 158–159: Details from Dead or Alive? (www.dead-or-alive.org).

p. 160: Details from Dead or Alive? and HarperCollins (www.harpercollins.com). Quote from Sylvia Plath, "Edge," *Ariel*, 1965. Plath's suicide echoed that of poet Hart Crane, who killed himself at 32 by jumping off a steamship.

p. 161: Details from IMDb and Michael Epstein and Thomas Lennon, *The Battle Over Citizen Kane,* WGBH Boston Video, 1996. Apparently, Welles did indeed eat 18 hot dogs in one go.

pp. 162–163: Details and quote from IMDb.

p. 164: Stat from "NFL Nation Fast Facts," *ESPN The Magazine,* Feb. 4, 2002.

p. 165: Details from Larry Schwartz, "Jim Brown Was Hard to Bring Down," ESPN.com, and IMDb. In point of fact, the Cleveland Browns were founded in 1946 by Mickey McBride, while Brown University was founded in 1764 based on a charter drafted by James Manning and the Rev. Ezra Stiles.

p. 166: Alexander details from Williams College and Mohammed Yasin, "The Greek Connection," *The Dawn* (www.dawn.com). Buceph'alos details from Bibliomania.com and E. Cobham Brewer, *Dictionary of Phrase and Fable,* 1898.

p. 167: Thirty Years War stat from *Columbia Encyclopedia,* 6th Edition, 2001. The Thirty Years War raged from 1618 to 1648, primarily in Central Europe. Ox lifespan stat from "Animal Lifespans," *Encyclopaedia Britannica,* 1961.

pp. 168–169: Jobs details from "Steve Jobs Timeline," SFGate.com. Murphy details from Peter Travers, "*Boomerang:* The *Rolling Stone* Review," *Rolling Stone,* No. 636, and IMDb. Ringwald details from IMDb and Ben Brantley, "Still Licentious, but Freshly Vulnerable Too," *New York Times,* Jan. 16, 2002. Jordan details from "Michael Jordan Chronology," *USA Today,* Sept. 25, 2001 and 23Jordan.com. Locklear details from IMDb. Ruth details from David Schoenfield, "Most Ignominious Moments in Yankees' History," ESPN.com, 2000, and BabeRuth.com.

p. 171: Stat from "Five Year Survival Rates," U.S. Census, April 1996; stat is middle mortality assumption in 2000–2005 for people ages 30–34 living to ages 35–39.

Some quotes were first uncovered on the website Bartleby.com.

In the beginning, there was chaos. And then there was Lisa Bankoff. Thanks to her and Patrick Price at ICM for making it happen.

Our undying gratitude to the Crown BOA squad: top gun Annik LaFarge, heavy-hitter Pete Fornatale, secret weapon Dorianne Steele, and special agents Linnea Knollmueller, Jill Flaxman, Kate Harris, and Brian Belfiglio.

Thanks, too, to Anne Ursu and Ann Campbell for essential early-stage help.

Thanks to friends and family who read previous iterations of this book and made it better: Salma Abdelnour, Jacob Albertson, Jason Albertson, Ellen and Mark Albertson, Dan Barcan, Jed Bennett, Andy Bernstein, Mike Burger, Charley Dane, Maggie Edelman, D. J. Haddad, Joey Liao, Alison Lobron, J. J. McArdle, Marshall Miller, Christina Nicosa, Alexis Palmer, Michael Oates Palmer, Ken Schwartz, Nicola Sheara, Matt Shepatin, Hiro Shinohara, Dorian Solot, Roslyn Stahl, Carol Steele, George Steele, Chris Stewart, Anne Ursu, The Shakespeare Road Van Giesons (especially C. J.), and Dov Weinstein.

We would also like to recognize Sherry-Lehmann, the F train, Titania, Yoshimi, Good World, Google, and Lil' Frankie for all their hard work.

Special thanks to our families for the best 30 years of our lives. Also, JVG thanks Xina, because he does.

JOSHUA ALBERTSON, LOCKHART STEELE, and **JONATHAN VAN GIESON** have created or produced a variety of media projects, including web-based reality game Hide/Seek/NYC, *The Pharmer's Almanac,* "Buddy" Cianci: the musical, and SiteSherpa. Their next book in the series, *Book of Ages 40,* will be published in 2004. They live in New York City.

JOSHUA ALBERTSON
Turns 30: 10/28/2004

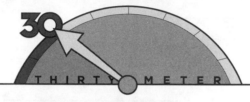

Throws up grape juice in third grade classroom
LOW: Age 8

High school homecoming king
HIGH: Age 17

LOCKHART STEELE
Turns 30: 1/9/2004

"Kegs incident"
LOW: Age 20

Gentrifies Avenue C
HIGH: Age 23

JONATHAN VAN GIESON
Turns 30: 3/31/2004

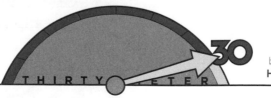

Removed from tree by police
LOW: Age 18

Eats entire two-pound bag of M&Ms
HIGH: Age 19

Autographs

Autographs

HANKERING FOR MORE?

87% can't wait to take the "How 30 Are You?" interactive quiz

75% plan to send **free 30th birthday e-cards** to friends

92% are dying for **the scoop on other landmark ages**, like 40

WWW.BOOKOFAGES.COM

at age 30... or anytime!